I AM *Highly* FAVOURED

With over 400 prayer points
that can change your life

FATAI KASALI

I Am Highly Favoured

Copyright © 2024 Fatai Kasali

The author has asserted his right to be identified as the author of this work in accordance with the Copyright, Designs and Patents Act 1988.

All rights reserved. No part of this publication may be reproduced, stored in a retrieval system, or transmitted in any form or by any means, electronic, mechanical, photocopying, recording or otherwise, without the prior permission of the author.

All Scripture quotations, unless otherwise indicated, are taken from the Holy Bible, King James Version, Cambridge University Press, Oxford University Press, HarperCollins and the Queen's Printers.

Scripture quotations marked 'Phillips' are taken from The New Testament in Modern English, copyright © 1958, 1959, 1960 J.B. Phillips and 1947, 1952, 1955, 1957 The MacMillian Company, New York. Used by permission. All rights reserved.

Published in the United Kingdom by Glory Publishing

ISBN: 978-1-7385361-3-9

Acknowledgements

To God be the glory for the grace to write this book. I give God all the praise and adoration for inspiring me through His Spirit to write this book.

I want to especially appreciate my family and everyone God has used to contribute, in one way or another, to the success of this work. I say a big thank you to all of you.

Introduction

Luke 1:28 (KJV): *And the angel came in unto her, and said, Hail, thou that art highly favoured, the Lord is with thee: blessed art thou among women.*

Favour can be defined as the grace of God upon His children. Favour and grace are used interchangeably because grace is the unmerited favour of God. Therefore, 'favour' means to enjoy acceptance, goodwill, and special treatment. Favour grants you what is denied to other people. Therefore, there is no fairness, equity, or equality in favour. When the principle of favour is introduced, men are treated differently. God's decision to show you favour has nothing to do with your personal qualifications or attributes. This is why you may discover that those more qualified than you are denied the same privilege God gives you on a platter of gold. Favour from God is totally a product of God's sovereignty. The good news is that our God is compassionate and never ignores a cry for help or favour. The only thing that can make any man qualify for divine favour is God's compassion.

Ephesians 2:7-9 (KJV): *That in the ages to come he might shew the exceeding riches of his grace in his kindness toward us through Christ Jesus. For by grace are ye saved through faith; and that not of yourselves: it is the gift of God: Not of works, lest any man should boast.*

The above Bible verses indicate that God, in His favour, saved us from damnation coming upon this world. He saved us out of His mercy. He showed us favour. We paid nothing to God to save us. In His favour, God saved us from this dirty world. What qualified us to be saved while the same God did not save others in the world? It was God's favour that saved us, not our qualifications. On this side of eternity, we will never know why God saved some people out of this world and left others in their mess. Favour is never fair, and neither does it have equality.

Romans 5:8 (KJV): *But God commendeth his love toward us, in that, while we were yet sinners, Christ died for us.*

The above Bible verse teaches us that we paid God nothing for Him to show us favour. His favour was given to us free of charge.

Fortunately, the same principle of favour is still at work in the kingdom of God.

God's favour is independent of your goodness, holiness, perfection, or self-righteousness. Therefore, when you ask God for favour, don't boast of your personal qualifications or attributes before Him.

Luke 4:25-26 (KJV): *But I tell you of a truth, many widows were in Israel in the days of Elias, when the heaven was shut up three years and six months, when great famine was throughout all the land; But unto none of them was Elias sent, save unto Sarepta, a city of Sidon, unto a woman that was a widow.*

In the above Bible verses, the Lord Jesus said many Israelite women were widows during the time of famine, but God sent help to only one widow in the city of Sidon. God is sovereign, and He does as He pleases in His sovereignty. That is why you should never count yourself out in any situation because God is a sovereign God, and nobody can question Him when He decides to favour you.

Luke 2:52 (KJV): *And Jesus increased in wisdom and stature, and in favour with God and man.*

The Bible verse above shows that Jesus' success in life could be traced to favour.

If Jesus could not succeed without favour, you also can't succeed in life without favour. Therefore, in every situation, ask God to show you favour.

As a believer, consider salvation a call into a life of favour.

Genesis 41:14 (KJV): *Then Pharaoh sent and called Joseph, and they brought him hastily out of the dungeon: and he shaved himself, and changed his raiment, and came in unto Pharaoh.*

In the above story, King Pharaoh sent for Joseph while in prison. It was a call to come into a life of favour. That call was an invitation to many good things that happened to Joseph in Egypt.

The day you gave your life to Jesus, you answered a call into the life of divine favour. Salvation is a call into a life full of divine favour. Every good thing you will enjoy from the Lord comes to you free. As your salvation is not a wage but a gift from the Lord, the life you will live in salvation is filled with the favour of God that brings you free blessings from the Lord.

In salvation, the Lord calls you out of a life of dream stagnation into a life of dream fulfilment, where all your desires are realised. Salvation is a call out of a life of bondage into a life of freedom where all the chains and shackles the enemy is using to tie you down are broken. Salvation calls you out of a life of weakness into strength and power. In salvation, the Lord calls you out of a life of limitation into unlimited enlargement, where you have space for unlimited enlargement in destiny. In salvation, you are called never to be small. The day you answered the call of God into salvation, you came out of a life of shame into a life full of glory and honour. In His favour, the Lord saved you by calling you out of a life of unfruitfulness into fruitfulness, where things that once failed to work for you will begin to succeed. Salvation is free. It is a call out of a life of slavery into that of dominion. Salvation is a call out of a life of insecurity to that of security. You are called out of a life of impossibility to that of possibilities.

Your salvation is a call from a life of condemnation into justification, where you enjoy every good thing without payment. That is a favour from heaven.

You paid nothing to be saved and will not pay anything to walk in divine favour. It is a gift from heaven. What made you qualify for salvation also makes you qualify for divine favour. As you progress in salvation, always ask God for divine favour because it is all you need to enjoy a life of unlimited possibilities.

You are holding in your hand a book that can turn your destiny around for good. This book is written to enlighten believers about the supremacy of God's favour over every requirement and demand life may place on them before they can rise in destiny.

God introduced the principle of favour to remove the gaps between the weak and the mighty, born-rich and born-poor, less privileged and much privileged, able and disabled. Life has been so good to some people because they were born into a life of opportunities, while countless others were born into a life of struggles. There are people in this life who have never tasted poverty, while many others are born into poverty, grow up in poverty, and die in poverty. The disparities between men are beyond words. Despite all these differences between men, we are all created by the same loving God.

In order to help the less privileged, God, in His wisdom, introduced the idea of divine favour. With favour, the less privileged can become much more privileged, and the less fortunate can become the most fortunate. Your understanding of the blessings of favour will make you never consider yourself unfortunate in every situation you can find yourself in or life can put you into. With favour, there is nothing good you can't achieve in life. Whenever you are in an unfortunate position, cry to God for favour. Favour removes every barrier and limitation.

This book exposes a limitless number of advantages that favour can bring you. Therefore, ask God for favour whenever you find yourself on the wrong side of life. What favour can do for you is unlimited. The last chapter of this book contains many prayer points on divine favour. These prayer points can change the lives of readers. God bless you as you enjoy this book.

Contents

CHAPTER 1
Favour Can Make What Works Against Others Work for You 13

CHAPTER 2
Favour Can Turn Around for Your Good
What the Enemy Meant for Evil 15

CHAPTER 3
Favour Can Speak Well of You in Places That Matter 17

CHAPTER 4
Favour Can Make You an Effortless Winner 19

CHAPTER 5
Favour Can Give You Free What You Are Supposed to Pay For 21

CHAPTER 6
Favour Can Give You a Promotion That
Is Beyond Your Qualifications 23

CHAPTER 7
Favour Can Make You Noticeable to People That Matter 25

CHAPTER 8
Favour Can Make You Prosper in All Seasons 27

CHAPTER 9
Favour Can Make You Enter into the
Labours of Other People 29

CHAPTER 10
Favour Can Qualify You to Be a Distributor of God's Blessings 31

CHAPTER 11
Favour Can Give You Wisdom That Eludes Other People 33

CHAPTER 12
Favour Can Grant You Compensation
for the Losses You Suffered 35

CHAPTER 13
Favour Can Bring You Satisfaction 37

CHAPTER 14
Favour Can Arrest Your Destiny Helpers for Your Sake 39

CHAPTER 15
Favour Can Lead You to a Place of Better Things 41

CHAPTER 16
Favour Can Qualify You for Unexpected Pleasant Changes 43

CHAPTER 17
Favour Can Turn Curses into Blessings for You 45

CHAPTER 18
Favour Can Put You in an Advantageous Position 47

CHAPTER 19
Favour Can Turn a Stumbling Block
into a Stepping Stone for You 49

CHAPTER 20
Favour Can Turn Your Rejection into a Direction 51

CHAPTER 21
Favour Can Give You Freely What Other People Are Toiling For 53

CHAPTER 22
Favour Can Make You Recover Losses That Men Call Irrecoverable 55

CHAPTER 23
Favour Can Qualify You for Meteoric Promotion 57

CHAPTER 24
Favour Can Make You a Sought-Out Person 59

CHAPTER 25
Favour Can Turn Your Foolishness to Wisdom 61

CHAPTER 26
Favour Can Raise a Voice for You in Your Absence 63

CHAPTER 27
Favour Can Make You Come Out Stronger from Difficult Situations 65

CHAPTER 28
Favour Can Take You out of Impossible Pits 67

CHAPTER 29
Favour Can Dissolve Threats Meant to Come to Pass Against Your Life 69

CHAPTER 30
Favour Can Bring You Life 71

CHAPTER 31
Favour Can Fast-Forward Your Journey 73

CHAPTER 32
Favour Can Give You Victory over the
Secret Plot of the Enemy 75

CHAPTER 33
Favour Can Separate You from General Problems 77

CHAPTER 34
Favour Can Grant You an Upgrade at No Cost 79

CHAPTER 35
Favour Can Move You from One Level of Favour to Another 81

CHAPTER 36
Favour Can Cause Pleasant Coincidences for You 83

CHAPTER 37
Favour Can Cause Good Things to Seek for You 85

CHAPTER 38
Favour Can Make Your Destiny Helpers That Had
Forgotten You Remember You 87

CHAPTER 39
Favour Can Bring You Unceasing Help 89

CHAPTER 40
Favour Can Cut Off All the Enemies That Rise Against You 91

Prayers on Divine Favour 93

CHAPTER ONE

Favour Can Make What Works Against Others Work for You

Daniel 3:22-25 (KJV): *Therefore because the king's commandment was urgent, and the furnace exceeding hot, the flame of the fire slew those men that took up Shadrach, Meshach, and Abed-nego. And these three men, Shadrach, Meshach, and Abed-nego, fell down bound into the midst of the burning fiery furnace. Then Nebuchadnezzar the king was astonied, and rose up in haste, and spake, and said unto his counsellers, Did not we cast three men bound into the midst of the fire? They answered and said unto the king, True, O king. He answered and said, Lo, I see four men loose, walking in the midst of the fire, and they have no hurt; and the form of the fourth is like the Son of God.*

In the above story, the hotness of the fire that killed others made the three Hebrews cold. Favour can make what makes others lose to make you gain. Favour can make what works for the disadvantage of others work for your advantage.

In case you find yourself in a situation whereby things are working against other people, instead of you starting to expect the same treatment, cry to God for favour. Ask God to show you favour by making what works against others work in your favour. With His favour, the Lord can turn what disadvantages others into something that works to your advantage.

Favour causes God to distinguish you from the crowd. He can turn what demotes others into something that promotes you. The Lord can cause you to rejoice in what makes others sorrowful. The Lord can cause to work for your good what works for the evil of others. That is favour. Favour can provide you with direction where others find confusion. It can lead you out of difficulty in situations that bring others into difficulty. With favour, you can make gains where others make losses. What is not suitable for others can become suitable for you due to favour. A manager who does not listen to others' unhappiness can listen to yours due to favour. The person who is always at war with others can be at peace with you due to favour.

In general, in a negative situation, ask God for favour.

Prayer: Father, let your favour cause situations that work against others to work for me, in Jesus' name.

CHAPTER TWO

Favour Can Turn Around for Your Good What the Enemy Meant for Evil

Genesis 50:20 (KJV): *But as for you, ye thought evil against me; but God meant it unto good, to bring to pass, as it is this day, to save much people alive.*

In Genesis 39, the brothers of Joseph sold him into slavery. Their intention was clear—to kill his dream and terminate his life without using their own hands.

Fortunately, when Joseph reached Egypt, instead of his life fulfilling the wish of his hateful brothers, divine favour took over. Joseph started having favour with every man he contacted. Furthermore, for every hindrance that came his way in Egypt, divine favour turned it around for his good.

Favour can turn it for your good, every evil plan and device of the wicked concerning your life. When you find yourself under the grip of the wicked, instead of losing hope, start crying to God to grant you favour and turn for your good all that the enemy meant for your evil. With divine favour working for you, the persecutors cannot succeed in terminating your destiny, and all the enemy's plans will come to nought. As God's favour is on your side, rest assured that whoever rises against you to hinder your progress will only promote your advancement. If the enemy puts you inside a pit, God's favour will draw you out. God's favour can terminate every terminator that wants to terminate your life. When the brethren of Joseph sold him into slavery to terminate his destiny, favour made their plot to promote it instead. No matter how strong the wickedness of the wicked is against you, favour can make it fail.

Any tempter assigned against you will fail when favour is on your side. Every arrow the enemy fires at you shall return to sender, and any wrong accusation levelled against you shall not succeed.

When favour is on your side, your helper of destiny that has forgotten you will remember you. With favour, injustice is defeated, and liars are disgraced. With favour, no power can deny you the opportunity or silence you.

Are you under the attack of haters? It is time for you to cry to God to grant you favour and turn around for your good all that the wicked meant for your evil.

Prayer: Father, let your favour turn around all that the enemy meant for my evil into good, in Jesus' name.

CHAPTER THREE

Favour Can Speak Well of You in Places That Matter

2 Samuel 5:1-3 (KJV): *Then came all the tribes of Israel to David unto Hebron, and spake, saying, Behold, we are thy bone and thy flesh. Also in time past, when Saul was king over us, thou wast he that leddest out and broughtest in Israel: and the LORD said to thee, Thou shalt feed my people Israel, and thou shalt be a captain over Israel. So all the elders of Israel came to the king to Hebron; and king David made a league with them in Hebron before the LORD: and they anointed David king over Israel.*

In the above story, all the elders of Israel came to make David a king over them.

There are many questions from the above story, such as:

- Among the elders, who started the discussion of making David a king over the whole nation?
- Who arranged the meeting before they came to David?
- Who presented the credible argument that David could be their king?
- Who convinced other elders and unanimously agreed to make David a king?
- How did the elders know that the whole nation would accept their choice of David as a king?

The only answer to the above question is that favour did it.

Favour has a voice, and everyone will concur when it speaks for you. Favour can influence people who matter to your destiny to unite for your sake.

Favour can rise for you, men who can lift you to a greater height. With favour on your side, great men can rally round to fight for your interest. Favour can make people that matter to be pleased with you. When favour puts your interest into the heart of men, they become willing to work for your good. Are you in a situation whereby you need approval or general acceptance from certain people, an organisation, or a panel? Instead of losing hope, cry to God for favour because favour can cause general acceptance for you in places that matter. You cannot experience rejection or have people who matter ignore you if favour is on your side.

Favour has a voice, and when it speaks for you, no ear can ignore the sound. Even in a situation whereby your good deeds have been forgotten, favour can wake up the people in charge of your reward.

Favour can defend you in secret places, and it is able to create a voice among great men for you. Favour can't be on your side, and you will be forgotten forever.

Prayer: Father, let your favour speak well of me in places that matter, in Jesus' name.

CHAPTER FOUR

Favour Can Make You an Effortless Winner

Exodus 14:24-25 (KJV): *And it came to pass, that in the morning watch the LORD looked unto the host of the Egyptians through the pillar of fire and of the cloud, and troubled the host of the Egyptians, And took off their chariot wheels, that they drave them heavily: so that the Egyptians said, Let us flee from the face of Israel; for the LORD fighteth for them against the Egyptians.*

In the above story, God fought for Israel against the Egyptians, and the Egyptians themselves confessed that God was fighting for Israel against them. Israel defeated their strong enemies without effort—God did it all for them. That was favour. Favour helps you to win battles you did not engage in. You become an effortless winner—a winner who wins without any effort. When someone receives favour, the victory others achieved through fight will come to them without struggle.

Are you facing any battle? If yes, you don't need to worry about fighting it. Instead, ask God for favour. When the favour of God fights for you, your victory is certain, and you will become an effortless winner. You can save the energy and resources you would have expended on this fight for something better.

With favour on your side, your path to victory becomes smooth and sure. Favour makes God take over your battle and save you from unnecessary effort and worry. Favour makes God to be your strength and strategy in battle.

Favour makes you do valiantly in battle. Favour makes your rising painless, and you enjoy victory without any injury; after all, you don't participate in the battle. With favour, you can enjoy golden achievement without struggle as the Lord becomes your strongman in the battle of your life. As favour makes the Lord fight your battle for you, He takes care of all those who want to trouble you. Even those who want to fight you will soon discover that it is not you that they are fighting but God. Favour brings you victory greater than your strength, and every complication is removed from your path because the Lord's favour fights for you. Never be afraid of any battle; instead, ask God for favour to fight for you and give you victory greater than your efforts. With favour on your side, you will go stronger in battle instead of weaker.

Prayer: Father, let your favour make me an effortless winner in every battle of my life, in Jesus' name.

CHAPTER FIVE

Favour Can Give You Free What You Are Supposed to Pay For

2 Kings 4:8-11 (KJV): *And it fell on a day, that Elisha passed to Shunem, where was a great woman; and she constrained him to eat bread. And so it was, that as oft as he passed by, he turned in thither to eat bread. And she said unto her husband, Behold now, I perceive that this is an holy man of God, which passeth by us continually. Let us make a little chamber, I pray thee, on the wall; and let us set for him there a bed, and a table, and a stool, and a candlestick: and it shall be, when he cometh to us, that he shall turn in thither. And it fell on a day, that he came thither, and he turned into the chamber, and lay there.*

In the above story, Elisha often enjoyed free accommodation with meals many times from a family in Shunem. This offer came from this family without Elisha asking for it. Favour gave Elisha what he was supposed to pay for.

When someone walks in favour, he will not pay for many things others pay for. Favour strengthens your purchasing power to buy many things cheaply or without payment. With favour, you can buy a nation without a penny.

The Lord's favour can grant you free access to essential support that your life needs as a family. In the above Bible verses, God gave Elisha the critical support he needed for his assignment in the land.

Do you lack essential support in some regions of your life? Instead of you considering quitting, why don't you ask God for favour? It will supply every essential thing that you need for free. Favour can open the door to every support your life needs for a better living. Favour can give you free access to good treatment, so people will treat you well and bless you with their free substances. With favour, promotion can be delivered to you on a platter of gold, and you can have free access to comfort. Favour can give you free access to places where your burden will be lifted, and all your needs are met. Favour is able to order your steps to places where free blessings are waiting for you. Whatever you need for life that you don't have is available somewhere, but only favour can bring you there. With favour, you can enjoy the labour of another man for free. As a child of God, never accept your lack as a cross. Instead, pray to God for the favour that will bring you to places of free provisions.

Prayer: Father, let your favour bring me to places where I will enjoy provisions without a cost, in Jesus' name.

CHAPTER SIX

Favour Can Give You a Promotion That Is Beyond Your Qualifications

Judges 6:12-15 (KJV): *And the angel of the LORD appeared unto him, and said unto him, The LORD is with thee, thou mighty man of valour. And Gideon said unto him, Oh my Lord, if the LORD be with us, why then is all this befallen us? and where be all his miracles which our fathers told us of, saying, Did not the LORD bring us up from Egypt? but now the LORD hath forsaken us, and delivered us into the hands of the Midianites. And the LORD looked upon him, and said, Go in this thy might, and thou shalt save Israel from the hand of the Midianites: have not I sent thee? And he said unto him, Oh my Lord, wherewith shall I save Israel? behold, my family is poor in Manasseh, and I am the least in my father's house.*

In the above story, God promoted Gideon to a leadership position, and Gideon said he has no family, personal, social, or tribal qualification to be chosen for such a position. Truly, Gideon was right, but favour made him qualified.

Have you written yourself off from certain promotions or elevations in life? Have you been told you don't possess everything required to rise to a certain height in life? Instead of considering yourself unfortunate, why can't you ask God for the favour that will give you the promotion you don't qualify for?

With favour on your side, you can qualify for a promotion beyond your qualifications. Unexpected promotions can come to you when you walk in favour. Favour can give you a promotion far above your life experience—a promotion that disgraces your curriculum vitae.

When favour speaks for you, academic achievement is set aside. Favour sidetracks demand for the qualification you don't possess. Favour takes you above your fellow and disappoints those who have set a limit for your rising in life. With favour, you can never be unfortunate or be on the wrong side of destiny. Favour bridges any gap between where you are and where you are supposed to be in life. Favour converts your limitations to elevation, where everything that wants to limit you starts lifting you up. When favour speaks for you, what you consider a limiting factor is used as a reason for your lifting. Favour makes life treat you based on your heavenly identity and qualifications, not earthly ones. When heaven says you are qualified for a thing, favour says, *so shall it be* to the earth, and the earth concurs. It is time for you to aspire to reach a greater height, irrespective of your limitations. It is all about favour and not the demand of the world.

Prayer: Father, give me a favour that will give me a promotion beyond my qualifications, in Jesus' name.

CHAPTER SEVEN

Favour Can Make You Noticeable to People That Matter

1 Samuel 16:17-18 (KJV): *And Saul said unto his servants, Provide me now a man that can play well, and bring him to me. Then answered one of the servants, and said, Behold, I have seen a son of Jesse the Bethlehemite, that is cunning in playing, and a mighty valiant man, and a man of war, and prudent in matters, and a comely person, and the LORD is with him.*

In the above story, among many young people in Israel, only David, the servant of King Saul, could play for the king's healing. A boy who had been hiding in the desert following animals suddenly became noticeable to the king of the land. This can only be God's favour at work.

When God's favour is upon you, people who matter will notice you, even among many millions. Favour brings you out where the enemy is hiding you.

The favour of God will take you out of darkness into the limelight.

Are you concerned that the world does not take notice of your potential? Do you feel you are going through life unnoticed by those who matter? Are you feeling forgotten in life?

Instead of feeling discouraged that life is treating you like an outcast, cry to God to give you favour that will make you noticeable to people who matter.

Favour can break the dominion of the power of darkness hiding you from the world. Wherever the enemy hides you to prevent you from fulfilling your destiny, the power of divine favour can overturn and uncover it. No power can cover your glory when God's favour is at work in your life. God's favour can remove every dark covering over your life.

Any covering over your potential is removable by the power of divine favour.

With the favour of God on your side, any dark shadow journey with you can be removed, and God's favour will bring you to the place where you will shine for God. The favour of God can announce your gifting to the world, and all those who think you are empty will now discover that you are loaded with heavenly treasures. Favour of God can give you opportunities to show and develop your potential and take out of the way any evil boss hindering your professional development. It is time for the world to discover that you carry solutions to their problems. Ask God for favour, for by it, you can become a person the world can't ignore.

Prayer: Father, give me a favour that will make me noticeable to people that matter, in Jesus' name.

CHAPTER EIGHT

Favour Can Make You Prosper in All Seasons

Psalm 1:1-3 (KJV): *Blessed is the man that walketh not in the counsel of the ungodly, nor standeth in the way of sinners, nor sitteth in the seat of the scornful. But his delight is in the law of the LORD; and in his law doth he meditate day and night. And he shall be like a tree planted by the rivers of water, that bringeth forth his fruit in his season; his leaf also shall not wither; and whatsoever he doeth shall prosper.*

The above Bible verses indicate that it is possible for a person to prosper in all seasons, irrespective of changes in and around him. When a person receives favour from God, changes in circumstances will not hinder his performance. In fact, whatever changes occur will be suitable for his good achievements.

For example, a change of government, a change in leadership at the place of work, age-related changes, or any other changes will not be able to hinder the good performance of a man walking in favour of God. Wherever you put a person that carries favour, he will still perform well.

Are you concerned that certain changes in and around you may hinder your success? Are you worried that you may lose control of situations due to the unpredictability of life? There is good news for you. With God's favour upon your life, whatever changes are happening will only advance your success. Therefore, ask God to release your life more to His favour. God's favour can turn around for your good in any situation that wants to regulate your performance. Favour can eliminate every possibility of failure from your life. Favour of God can create wellness around you, forcing every situation to work for your success. Divine favour is so powerful that it can place you far above failure and make you unlimited in success. Favour can grant you good performance that any change cannot hinder. With God's favour on you, every evil occurrence becomes forbidden, and your life is shielded from every negative incidence. Favour ensures that life remains easy, irrespective of any form of change. God's grace that comes with favour ensures that all things remain easy despite all the changes. With favour, a good seed can't die, and every factor connected to your work makes it succeed. Never be afraid of any form of change because you carry on your life's divine favour that makes every season beautiful for you.

Prayer: Father, give me the favour that will make me prosper in all seasons, in Jesus' name.

CHAPTER NINE

Favour Can Make You Enter into the Labours of Other People

John 4:38 (KJV): *I sent you to reap that whereon ye bestowed no labour: other men laboured, and ye are entered into their labours.*

According to the above Bible verse, entering another person's labour means reaping the harvest due to another person. It means that a person can reap where he did not sow. With God's favour on you, you can take over houses you did not build, inherit fields you did not plant, and enjoy pleasures from another man's labour. There are many testimonies of people who have taken over businesses established by other men as the owners of such businesses willingly release them. That is a favour at work.

It is good to be hard-working, but it is more beneficial to walk in favour. With favour, you can enjoy harvests far greater than your own harvest. The favour of God can qualify you to enjoy the harvest from another man's labour. Life becomes easier with less struggle if other men work and their labours are transferred to you. The reality of this life is that nobody owns anything because all things belong to God, and God has the right to distribute the treasures of the earth as He wishes. Therefore, if you find favour with God, He may choose to transfer the fruit of another man's labours to you. With God's favour on you, your steps can be ordered to places where you will reap without sowing and receive the profits due to another man. In His sovereignty, God can redistribute wealth and riches for your sake. Favour can cause shaking in places that matter to profit you. The blessings other people worked for can be transferred to you. The throne of honour set up for someone can be given to you because you are walking in divine favour. Favour can raise able men to serve your interest, and you will begin to enjoy unusual support you did not work for. It is possible for the Lord to give you the inheritance of another man. When you begin to enjoy pleasures you did not labour for, don't trace it to your hard work but to divine favour. When you occupy top positions created for other men, don't trace it to your dedication but to divine favour. When you notice that men come to you willingly to bless you with their substances, don't trace it to your generosity but divine favour. When good things are being brought to you on a platter of gold, don't trace it to your prayer but to divine favour. Divine favour makes other people work for your comfort. Whenever you notice that your harvest is not commensurate with your work, ask God to give you the favour that will make you enter into another man's labour.

Prayer: Father, give me the favour that will make me enter other people's labours, in Jesus' name.

CHAPTER TEN

Favour Can Qualify You to Be a Distributor of God's Blessings

John 6:11 (KJV): *And Jesus took the loaves; and when he had given thanks, he distributed to the disciples, and the disciples to them that were set down; and likewise of the fishes as much as they would.*

In the story above, Jesus chose disciples to distribute blessings to the hungry crowd. It was the favour of God that made disciples qualified to occupy such a position. The Lord Jesus chose them to be His disciples, not because they were the most qualified in Israel, but because they found favour with God.

It has been God's tradition to place His blessings in the custody of individuals and distribute them to people. God is always looking for someone to use to distribute His blessings to His people. The favour of God can qualify you to be the vessel God will use to distribute His blessings to His people.

Are you living based on the generosity of other people in your life? Are you in a position where your survival depends on the businesses established by other people? If God can make you depend economically on the business established by other people, the same God is able to put you in a position whereby other people will depend on you for their economic survival.

Divine favour can qualify you as the distributor of God's blessings to people.

The Lord can place in your hands the needs of other people. God can place you in a position whereby God will lift many people through you. God's favour can turn your life into a storehouse for divine blessings such that the future needs of many are placed in your hands. The Lord's favour can give you blessings that overflow to other people. Irrespective of your present situation, divine favour can make you an employer of labour whereby you employ many people. Do not count yourself out of such greatness because anything is possible when divine favour is at work.

With favour on your side, you can become a channel of deliverance to those in the bondage of poverty because the anointing that breaks the yoke of poverty will come on you through divine favour. In His favour, the Lord can make you a joy to many generations as you become a lender to nations. You can become a helper of destiny to many people because divine favour has promoted you to a position where people will seek your help. With divine favour on you, you can become a river of blessings that never dries to many people.

Prayer: Father, give me the favour that will qualify me to be a distributor of your blessings, in Jesus' name.

CHAPTER ELEVEN

Favour Can Give You Wisdom That Eludes Other People

Daniel 2:23 (KJV): *I thank thee, and praise thee, O thou God of my fathers, who hast given me wisdom and might, and hast made known unto me now what we desired of thee: for thou hast now made known unto us the king's matter.*

In the story above, the king of Babylon had a dream, and none of his wise men could interpret it. The king declared that he would bless whoever could interpret the dream. The Almighty God then shut the door of wisdom against all the wise men of Babylon for the sake of Daniel, who later interpreted the dream and became the king's favourite.

This story teaches us that when someone walks in favour, you can have wisdom that eludes others so that you can have blessings that elude other people.

Are you struggling to stand out among the crowd of competitors? Instead of giving up, ask God for the wisdom to make you stand out among the crowd. With God's favour on you, you can receive the wisdom that will take you far above your fellows and make you unequal. With the wisdom of God in you, you can offer solutions beyond the reach of your competitors. The Lord can give you the wisdom to advertise you as a solution carrier to the world. Beloved, every employer wants to keep in their team solution carriers. When you become a solution carrier, your employer will prefer you above your fellows because you carry the wisdom they don't have. When the wisdom that eludes others is found in you, promotion beyond their reach comes to you. When you walk in favour, you can shine in wisdom and excel in life. When divine favour gives you access to the room of heavenly wisdom, you become unequal among your mates. The wisdom of heaven can make you become a helper to people who matter, such as your employer. Wisdom unlocks the door of possibilities and God's favour that will bring you to such a level. With the wisdom of God on you, you can become a consultant to great men, which can unlock the door of your destiny. Favour can release on you the wisdom to shine as a star in life, whereby every man wants to associate with you because they see the solutions to their problems in you. The wisdom of God makes the wind of uncommon acceptance blow in your direction, and where other people suffer rejection, you will experience acceptance. Whenever you find yourself among the crowd of competitors, pray to God to give you the wisdom they don't have so that you can do what they cannot. This is the path to lifting what is beyond others, and it is the way to stand out among the crowd of competitors.

Prayer: Father, give me the favour that will provide me with the wisdom that eludes other people, in Jesus' name.

CHAPTER TWELVE

Favour Can Grant You Compensation for the Losses You Suffered

2 Kings 8:5-6 (KJV): *And it came to pass, as he was telling the king how he had restored a dead body to life, that, behold, the woman, whose son he had restored to life, cried to the king for her house and for her land. And Gehazi said, My lord, O king, this is the woman, and this is her son, whom Elisha restored to life. And when the king asked the woman, she told him. So the king appointed unto her a certain officer, saying, Restore all that was hers, and all the fruits of the field since the day that she left the land, even until now.*

In the story above, the land taken from the Shunammite woman was returned with all the proceeds made on it when she was away. She received compensation for the losses she suffered. There would be many other people in the same situation in the land who could not receive any compensation for their losses. The difference is the favour from God. When the favour of God is upon you, you will not only recover all your losses, but you will also receive any dividends from it.

Are you being denied the recovery of your losses with dividends? Have you experienced losses like other people? Instead of accepting that what you have lost is irrecoverable, why can't you ask God for divine favour to recover your losses with dividends?

Divine favour can reverse every injustice you have suffered and recover for you every good thing you have lost. The Lord can give you favour such that all those who had cheated you will willingly return all your blessings to you in their custody. For your sake, divine favour can arrest all the thieves that have stolen from your life. Thieves can return to you all they had stolen from your life when God's favour speaks for you. Divine favour can arrange pleasant coincidences for the sake of your recovery. With divine favour, your denied promotion can be released unto you, and you can be satisfied with justice.

In His favour, the Lord can lead you to places where compensations are waiting for you, and through the divine ordering of steps, you can recover all your losses. With favour upon your life, the Lord can raise a capable helper of restoration for you that will promote recovery of all your losses. With God's favour upon your life, every strong man keeping your blessings in their custody can willingly release them to you. In His favour, the Lord can turn the story of your losses into that of abundant gains.

Prayer: Father, give me a favour that will grant me compensation for my losses, in Jesus' name.

CHAPTER THIRTEEN

Favour Can Bring You Satisfaction

Deuteronomy 33:23 (KJV): *And of Naphtali he said, O Naphtali, satisfied with favour, and full with the blessing of the LORD: possess thou the west and the south.*

In the story above, the tribe of Naphtali received the allocation of land that can be described as a land of good tidings—a land of great fertility and blessings. This tribe did not fight for such land, but divine favour remembered them and gave it to them.

There is a God that, in His favour, can make the best come to you. When men are distributing blessings, divine favour can make you receive the best among those blessings. When positions are allocated to people, divine favour can ensure that you receive the best of the positions. In His favour, the Lord can give you blessings that will satisfy you such that you lack nothing good. There is a provision that sorts you out so that you are fully satisfied. There are treasures that, when they come to you, you will not only have joy, but you will experience overflowing joy. Are you dissatisfied with the situation in your life? Are you dissatisfied with your job, business, and other sources of your provisions? If you can ask God to satisfy you with favour, your story will improve. Divine favour can bring you to a level whereby all your expectations are satisfied and established. The Lord can even exceed all your expectations. He can give you provisions that are far beyond your experience. With God's favour on you, you can enjoy pleasures and blessings that make you lack nothing. In God's favour, you can be full of blessings and overflow. The Lord can lead you to situations that will give you testimonies of nothing missing or broken. The Lord can make all you touch appear as good as you anticipated. Divine favour removes imperfection and promotes excellence in provisions.

While other people struggle to gain the best of provisions, favour can bring you the best among the provisions for free. When favour is set into motion for your sake, the wind of heaven will start blowing in your direction, the best of the best among the blessings.

Prayer: Father, give me the favour that will bring me all-round satisfaction, in Jesus' name.

CHAPTER FOURTEEN

Favour Can Arrest Your Destiny Helpers for Your Sake

1 Samuel 16:11 (KJV): *And Samuel said unto Jesse, Are here all thy children? And he said, There remaineth yet the youngest, and, behold, he keepeth the sheep. And Samuel said unto Jesse, Send and fetch him: for we will not sit down till he come hither.*

In the story above, Samuel tells Jesse that he will not sit down until David arrives. Samuel's attention was arrested for the sake of David.

When you find favour with God, He is able to arrest all the helpers of destiny He has appointed for your sake. They will not rest until they help you.

With divine favour on you, irrespective of location, your destiny helpers can arise, searching for you, and they will not relax until they find and help you.

Are you in desperate need of a helper? Are you struggling alone? Instead of quitting, ask God to arrest your destiny helpers so that wherever they may be, they will not rest until they locate and help you. Life goes better when you have suitable helpers serving your interests.

Divine favour will not let rest all those that carry your blessings until they release them to you. Favour will not let those who carry your blessings elude you. Favour of God is able to keep awake all your helpers that the enemy has made to sleep over your case or forget you.

When divine favour is upon you, the Lord will give grace to your helpers for your sake to pay every price necessary for helping you so that those who could not help you in the past can now assist you. The Lord can assist your helpers in helping you, such that any power troubling your helpers to hinder them from helping you is broken.

Divine favour can bring the Lord to a standstill for your sake, all those whom God had assigned to lift you up in destiny. You can't walk in favour and suffer destiny failure. The Lord can tune the heart of your helpers to favour you. Favour makes the Lord command all your destiny helpers to help fulfil your destiny. Divine favour can make someone arise and fight for you where you were once rejected. With divine favour on your life, the Lord can send on an errand for your sake those who will make a way for you in life. Furthermore, divine favour can make God send His word into the hearts of those who hate you to start loving you and help you in destiny.

As you walk in favour, God can send His angels to places that matter to help you fulfil your destiny. Any evil stone that needs to be rolled away will be removed because you walk in God's favour.

Prayer: Father, give me the favour that will arrest all my destiny helpers for my sake, in Jesus' name.

CHAPTER FIFTEEN

Favour Can Lead You to a Place of Better Things

1 Samuel 9:3 (KJV): *And the asses of Kish Saul's father were lost. And Kish said to Saul his son, Take now one of the servants with thee, and arise, go seek the asses.*

1 Samuel 9:16-17 (KJV): *To morrow about this time I will send thee a man out of the land of Benjamin, and thou shalt anoint him to be captain over my people Israel, that he may save my people out of the hand of the Philistines: for I have looked upon my people, because their cry is come unto me. And when Samuel saw Saul, the LORD said unto him, Behold the man whom I spake to thee of! this same shall reign over my people.*

In the above Bible verses, the donkey of Saul's father was lost, and he sent Saul to search for it, but Saul found something far better than the donkey he was searching for. He found the throne of glory because God sent Samuel to make him a king. Divine favour can lead you to find a thing far better than what you were searching for. God can give you a job that will bring you blessings far better than the job you are actually seeking. God can do things for you that are far better and bigger than you desire.

Are you trusting God for anything, and is delay making you weary? Fear not, because God may be planning something far better and bigger than what you are seeking.

Divine favour can lead you to a place of better blessing. God can send you blessings that are greater than your expectations. God can make your life far more beautiful than you had anticipated. Divine favour is able to direct and order your steps to a place of better blessings. God can bless your effort and bring you a reward far greater than you deserve.

When someone finds favour with God, divine favour can direct his steps to places of better resources where he will have good things in abundance. There is a place where you can enjoy support far better than your thoughts. There is a place for better achievements. There is a place of greater joy and peace. There is a place of better reports where better good news is awaiting you. There is a place for better experiences in God. Divine favour can lead and bring you to such places.

Prayer: Father, give me the favour that will lead and bring me to places of better things in life, in Jesus' name.

CHAPTER SIXTEEN

Favour Can Qualify You for Unexpected Pleasant Changes

Luke 5:4-7 (KJV): *Now when he had left speaking, he said unto Simon, Launch out into the deep, and let down your nets for a draught. And Simon answering said unto him, Master, we have toiled all the night, and have taken nothing: nevertheless at thy word I will let down the net. And when they had this done, they inclosed a great multitude of fishes: and their net brake. And they beckoned unto their partners, which were in the other ship, that they should come and help them. And they came, and filled both the ships, so that they began to sink.*

In the story above, the Lord Jesus chose Peter's boat, among many others that belonged to other fishermen. Peter did not invite Jesus, nor did he do anything to make Jesus choose his boat. That was divine favour.

With this favour, Peter's negative situation turned into a positive one, and his life experienced a complete turnaround.

When you find favour with God, He can decide to choose you to show to the world that He is able to cause a turnaround in anyone's situation, irrespective of how terrible the problem may be.

Are you in a terrible situation? Are you in desperate need of change? Instead of being anxious, ask God for the favour to turn around your situation.

When you find favour with God, He can change your song of failure to that of success, such that in the same place where your nets caught nothing, you will catch plenty of blessings. Divine favour can make God change your disappointment to an appointment, such that what the enemy meant for evil for you, the Lord will turn around for your good. With favour in your life, the Lord can change your darkness to light, and you can find a way out of your trouble. Favour will make God change your frustration to motivation by sending you blessings that encourage you. Favour can invite the hand of God to lift you up and take you out of the darkness the enemy has created around you. Divine favour can change your fear to boldness as your failed attempt can turn into a success. With favour, the Lord can change your evil advertisement to a positive one, such that those who witnessed your failure will also witness your success. You can be celebrated where you were once mocked. The Lord can change your negative experience into a positive one and your negative testimony into a positive testimony. Favour can give you an outcome that can change your self-doubt to self-confidence. Divine favour can do wonders in your life if you can ask for it and believe it.

Prayer: Father, give me the favour that will qualify me for unexpected, pleasant changes, in Jesus' name.

CHAPTER SEVENTEEN

Favour Can Turn Curses into Blessings for You

Nehemiah 13:2 (KJV): *Because they met not the children of Israel with bread and with water, but hired Balaam against them, that he should curse them: howbeit our God turned the curse into a blessing.*

From the above Bible verse, God's favour upon Israel turned the curse their enemies placed on them into blessings.

Whoever curses a person who carries divine favour only provokes God's blessing on him. Divine favour can't co-exist with a curse at the same place.

Are you being troubled by curses? Do you notice strange evil occurrences in your life? Fear not, but ask God for favour.

Divine favour can turn the curse of barrenness into the blessing of fruitfulness, and what has made you unfruitful can give way to God's fruitfulness. What has been causing you sorrow can start giving you an overflow of joy. With favour, the curse of death can be turned to blessings of long life, and whatever is assigned to cut short your life will fail. Favour can remove every fingerprint of the wicked in your life.

As you walk in favour, sickness can be turned into health. Sickness is a curse, but health is a blessing. With God's favour, whatever enemy has made you sick can receive health. The Lord's favour can turn poverty into riches, and the season of lack in your life can be terminated.

With God's favour in your life, rejection can be turned to acceptance, and every mark of hatred in your life can be removed. Rejection is a curse, but acceptance is a blessing. Any cycle of rejection can be removed when divine favour is provoked. In any area of your life where curses are hindering you, God's favour, when set in motion, will cause blessings to overthrow curses. With favour, the curse of failure can be turned into success, and stagnancy can become advancement. Where curses have made you irrelevant in life, divine favour can make you relevant, and you will become a sought-after person. As God's favour comes on you, prepare for a dance of joy. The favour of God eliminates forces that have been lowering your head, and enemies can become friends. You are set apart to walk in favour; therefore, no curse can hinder your well-being.

Prayer: Father, give me the favour that will turn every curse upon my life into blessings, in Jesus' name.

CHAPTER EIGHTEEN

Favour Can Put You in an Advantageous Position

2 Samuel 5:1-3 (KJV): *Then came all the tribes of Israel to David unto Hebron, and spake, saying, Behold, we are thy bone and thy flesh. Also in time past, when Saul was king over us, thou wast he that leddest out and broughtest in Israel: and the LORD said to thee, Thou shalt feed my people Israel, and thou shalt be a captain over Israel. So all the elders of Israel came to the king to Hebron; and king David made a league with them in Hebron before the LORD: and they anointed David king over Israel.*

In the story above, the elders of Israel came to make David king over the nations of Israel. The kingmakers focused on the attributes of David that he had that others did not have. At this time, there were still many men in the house of Saul and other parts of Israel whom the kingmakers could consider as competitors to David for this position. Ahead of a time like this, God has built for David an impressive, undeniable, and unequalled record of achievements that no one else could have in Israel. God has put David in an advantageous position over any possible competitors.

When you find favour with God, He will put you in an advantageous position that will be impossible for any of your competitors to satisfy. Life is full of competitions where we compete for many things in life against other candidates but with God's favour on us we will discover that we are in advantageous positions over our competitors, and we win in every race.

Are you afraid of competing for good things in life? Are you afraid you may be defeated when competing for good things in life? Do not be afraid, but ask God to put you in an advantageous position such that there are no competitors that would be able to compete with you.

With the favour of God upon your life, the Lord can build for you a record of achievements that will make you win against all your competitors. The Lord is able to put you in a position where you will have a victory that will be undeniable to your competitors. The light that refuses to shine for others can start shining for you. With divine favour on your life, the Lord can add beauty to your work that eludes others, causing your work to always stand out among others. The Lord is able to put in you the excellence that eludes others such that you become unequal among your peers. The invisible hand of God will push you ahead of all your competitors because you are walking in divine favour.

Prayer: Father, give me the favour that will put me in an advantageous position in all situations concerning my life, in Jesus' name.

CHAPTER NINETEEN

Favour Can Turn a Stumbling Block into a Stepping Stone for You

Genesis 50:20 (KJV): *But as for you, ye thought evil against me; but God meant it unto good, to bring to pass, as it is this day, to save much people alive.*

In the story above, the enemies of Joseph threw many stumbling blocks on his way to destroy his dream, but God's favour on him turned this to build up his dream. For example, when they sold him into slavery with the intention of destroying his dream, this promoted his dream significantly. Even when Joseph was later imprisoned, this also promoted his dream.

When God's favour is on you, every stumbling block is turned into a stepping stone, and what is supposed to bring you down will lift you up to the next level.

Are enemies throwing stumbling blocks in your way? Do not panic; rather, pray for divine favour to turn it into a stepping stone for you.

With God's favour on your life, the Lord can use it to build you up with what the enemy has designed to destroy you. The narrow road the enemy put you on can actually lead you to your divine destination.

The Lord can strengthen you through what the enemy has designed to weaken you. The Lord can turn any evil argument against your promotion around just to advance your promotion. Divine favour can make you laugh at all those boasting against you. With God's favour on your life, what is supposed to cause you a decrease in certain areas can actually promote your increase. What the enemy designed to hinder your divine favour can be used to advance you.

For those that the devil has chosen to destroy you, divine favour can make them build you up. With the favour of God, enemies can become friends.

Divine favour can give you direction in what the enemy has designed to confuse you. Arrangements the devil has developed to cause you shame can bring you honour because divine favour is at work in your life. Beloved, fear not every evil arrangement designed by the wicked to slow you down because divine favour can use the same evil arrangement to lift you up.

Prayer: Father, give me the favour that will turn every stumbling block the enemy has put in my way into a stepping stone for my lifting, in Jesus' name.

CHAPTER TWENTY

Favour Can Turn Your Rejection into a Direction

Judges 11:1-3 (KJV): *Now Jephthah the Gileadite was a mighty man of valour, and he was the son of an harlot: and Gilead begat Jephthah. And Gilead's wife bare him sons; and his wife's sons grew up, and they thrust out Jephthah, and said unto him, Thou shalt not inherit in our father's house; for thou art the son of a strange woman. Then Jephthah fled from his brethren, and dwelt in the land of Tob: and there were gathered vain men to Jephthah, and went out with him.*

In the above story, the brothers of Jephthah rejected and denied him his inheritance. This rejection made him run away from his father's house to another land, where he worked hard until he became a great man. His rejection probably challenged him to do better in life. His brothers, who rejected him, later sought his favour. If Jephthah was not rejected, he would not have found it necessary to relocate to another land where he worked and became great. With divine favour on you, God will allow every rejection you experience to point you in the right direction.

Are you facing rejection? If yes, accept it with joy because God's favour is on you to turn rejection into a direction for you. When men deny you a space, expect God's favour to create a better space for you in a far better place. When men decide to close a door against you, rejoice because divine favour on you will open a better door in a better place. Do not stand before a closed door crying, but move on with hope that the divine favour on you will open a far better door for you that nobody can close.

In many situations, God permits the enemy to take from us a lesser blessing that blindfolds us, not allowing us to see greater blessings. Therefore, take every rejection as a blessing and every closed door as a sign of a better door about to open. God's favour can turn curses into blessings, rejection into direction, refusal into acceptance, hatred into love, demotion into promotion, and negativity into positivity.

Whenever a door is closed in your life, note that God is about to open another door, and whenever you lose certain opportunities, rejoice because the Lord will send a better one. You will carry divine favour, and whatever the enemy throws at you for evil shall be turned to good for you.

Prayer: Father, give me the favour that will turn rejection into direction for me, in Jesus' name.

CHAPTER TWENTY-ONE

Favour Can Give You Freely What Other People Are Toiling For

Acts 8:18-20 (KJV): *And when Simon saw that through laying on of the apostles' hands the Holy Ghost was given, he offered them money, Saying, Give me also this power, that on whomsoever I lay hands, he may receive the Holy Ghost. But Peter said unto him, Thy money perish with thee, because thou hast thought that the gift of God may be purchased with money.*

In the above story, Simeon wanted to buy with money what God has freely given us. Truly, all we enjoy freely from the Lord is what many rich people of the world seek with a lot of money. God's favour gives us what most people toil and struggle to obtain freely.

Do you have a need that money can't buy? Do you have a need that money can buy, but you don't have enough cash for it?

Divine favour can freely give you what other people are struggling to obtain. God is able to give you the blessings your peers are toiling for in the world freely. Do not let your lack of strength discourage you from pursuing what others around the globe strive for through toil. You carry divine favour, which will make life easier for you than your peers.

Divine favour can deliver blessings to you beyond the reach of the world's people. The Lord can remove struggling and toiling from your life and end your days of wasted efforts.

Instead of struggling like the people of the world, the Lord can lead you to places where blessings await you. With divine favour, you can enjoy unusual generosity from the Lord. Do not expect life to be hard for you as it has been hard for your mates because you carry divine favour upon your life.

Divine favour can give you an effortless achievement in life whereby good things begin to pursue you instead of you pursuing them. Favour of God can grant you gifts money cannot buy, making life easier for you. What people of the world are struggling to obtain can come to you on a platter of gold because you carry God's favour on your life. When you face needs beyond your reach, ask God for favour. When you are pursuing blessings that only the mighty men of the world can obtain, ask God for favour. Divine favour can achieve for you what your ability can't.

Prayer: Father, give me the favour that will bring me blessings that others are toiling for, in Jesus' name.

CHAPTER TWENTY-TWO

Favour Can Make You Recover Losses That Men Call Irrecoverable

John 9:32 (KJV): *Since the world began was it not heard that any man opened the eyes of one that was born blind.*

In John 9, Jesus opened the eyes of a man born blind. When those who were not present when this miracle happened heard about it, they doubted the miracle and said it was impossible for a man born blind to regain his sight. To them, certain losses are irrecoverable.

Are you also experiencing losses men call irrecoverable?

When divine favour is at work in your life, whatever you might have lost to the enemy is recoverable. Such recovery will not happen by your strength but by the unlimited power of our gracious God.

Divine favour can make your situation defy human logic such that every wrong calculation the enemy has made concerning your life affairs fails. The negative conclusion of men concerning your situation can be disgraced because divine favour makes what men call impossible possible in your life.

With God's favour upon your life, what men call irreversible in your life can become reversible because our God is a reverser of the irreversible.

Has the enemy made anything crooked in your life? If yes, fear not because it shall be straightened with divine favour.

Divine favour is so limitless that if any law stands against the recovery of your losses, it will be set aside, and any law incapacitating your advancement will change for your sake.

Divine favour can set you up for a divine encounter that will make it possible for you to recover your losses described as irrecoverable by men. Therefore, regardless of how long you have lost something, never lose hope because you carry God's favour in your life. If there is a need for any spiritual robber that has stolen from your life to be arrested, divine favour can do it so that your blessing in their hands can be recovered. For your sake, the Lord can overthrow the storeroom of the enemy, where he keeps your stolen blessings. Whatever the enemy has stolen from you, the Lord knows where it is being kept, and when favour speaks for you before God, recovery is done on your behalf. With divine favour, there are no irrecoverable losses.

Prayer: Father, give me the favour to make me recover losses that men call irrecoverable, in Jesus' name.

CHAPTER TWENTY-THREE

Favour Can Qualify You for Meteoric Promotion

Genesis 41:39-42 (KJV): *And Pharaoh said unto Joseph, Forasmuch as God hath shewed thee all this, there is none so discreet and wise as thou art: Thou shalt be over my house, and according unto thy word shall all my people be ruled: only in the throne will I be greater than thou. And Pharaoh said unto Joseph, See, I have set thee over all the land of Egypt. And Pharaoh took off his ring from his hand, and put it upon Joseph's hand, and arrayed him in vestures of fine linen, and put a gold chain about his neck.*

In Genesis 41, Joseph rose speedily to a high position in Egypt. It was the same day he appeared before King Pharaoh when he was made the prime minister of Egypt and introduced to the whole nation. He was also given a woman to marry.

A meteoric promotion is a promotion that develops very speedily. When the favour of God speaks for you, your rising can happen so fast that the height you are supposed to reach in years can take place in months. Favour can give you a promotion that does not follow steps or happen gradually.

Are you stagnant? Fear not, because with divine favour, you can rise so quickly and speedily go ahead of all those who have gone ahead of you in life.

With divine favour, the height that took someone many years to reach can take a highly favoured person a few months. Favour can cause a promotion to bypass any laid-down procedure because it happens so fast that there isn't enough time to follow the usual procedure. Favour can remove any delay against your promotion so that what hinders others will not hinder your promotion. The Lord can grant you a promotion that does not follow common speed and time duration. Divine favour can fast-track your promotion, bringing a promotion that was meant for the future into the present. Divine favour speeds up occurrences of good things while removing every force of delay and arguments that drag down promotion. When you stay in a position for too long, ask God to grant you a meteoric promotion so that your lifting will happen quickly.

Prayer: Father, give me the favour that will grant me a speedy promotion in every facet of life, in Jesus' name.

CHAPTER TWENTY-FOUR

Favour Can Make You a Sought-Out Person

Isaiah 62:12 (KJV): *And they shall call them, The holy people, The redeemed of the LORD: and thou shalt be called, Sought out, A city not forsaken.*

In the above Bible verse, God promised oppressed Israel that they would be out of oppression and be embraced by those who once despised them.

When someone finds favour with God, he becomes a sought-after person—a person people desire.

Are you feeling isolated from the rest of the world? Are you facing rejection from some places?

If your answer is yes, fear not, because with divine favour, the people who once rejected you will start seeking you.

With divine favour, the Lord can break into pieces the power assigned to isolate you from those who carry your blessings. As a sought-after person, your blessings, destiny helper, breakthrough, joy, good news, promotion, glory, open door, and every good thing you need for a decent life will find you out. The good stuff you were denied access to will seek you out because divine favour is at work in your life. Divine favour can close every gap the enemy has created between yourself and your place of destiny fulfilment. Favour makes your helpers find you out, and every oppression your destiny is experiencing is removed.

Those looking down on you will be ashamed when the Lord exalts you in their sight. The same people who call you a failure and despise you will start seeking you because divine favour has turned situations around in your life. When divine favour makes your life beautiful to behold, your despisers will start seeking you to associate with you.

Furthermore, divine favour is so strong that it can remove every shadow the enemy has created around your life to hide your stars. If you are in a position whereby you are not well appreciated because your potential seems buried within you, ask God to activate favour upon your life to bring alive every buried potential inside of you. Whatever the enemy is using to make the world not notice your giftings and potential, favour can remove it and turn you into a sought-after person. Be assured that no evil power or personality will be able to hide you from being noticed by people who matter when God decides to favour you.

Prayer: Father, give me the favour to make me a sought-after person, in Jesus' name.

CHAPTER TWENTY-FIVE

Favour Can Turn Your Foolishness to Wisdom

1 Kings 5:7 (KJV): *And it came to pass, when Hiram heard the words of Solomon, that he rejoiced greatly, and said, Blessed be the LORD this day, which hath given unto David a wise son over this great people.*

In the above Bible verse, King Haram praised God for giving Solomon to David—a child King David had with Bathsheba, the former wife of Uriah.

When a man finds favour with God, his foolish act can produce results that glorify God's name. We don't always get everything right, but when we find favour with God, our errors become things that will bring glory to God's name.

When a man finds favour with God, his foolish act can be turned into a wise act, as his foolishness produces a better outcome.

Have you committed an error? Instead of worrying about an error you made, ask God for favour and use your error to glorify His name by turning your foolishness into wisdom for you. Don't hate yourself whenever you commit an error; just pray that God should use it for His glory. Our God is all-wise, such that He can turn around any potential negative outcome into a positive outcome for you. Through divine favour, those rejoicing over your mistake will be disappointed because the Lord will make your mistakes bring you a good outcome. As a carrier of divine favour, don't sorrow over any of your mistakes, irrespective of how serious they may appear, for the Lord can turn them around for your good. Mistakes that want to bring limitation into your life can be turned around by divine favour such that what's supposed to limit you can promote you. Errors caused by wrong assumptions that aim to hinder you can be turned around by divine favour. Mistakes due to blind spots can be turned around such that what is supposed to bring you harm can bring comfort. God can deal with things you did not see well that led you into error so that they end up becoming a blessing to you. With divine favour, the Lord can use your ignorance for His glory so that things you did not know will not hinder your destiny. The Lord can use your immaturity, insensitivity, unpreparedness, inexperience, and every other factor that made you commit errors for His glory. With divine favour, the wrong button you accidentally pressed will not destroy you but shall turn into blessings for you.

Prayer: Father, give me the favour that will turn my foolishness into wisdom, in Jesus' name.

CHAPTER TWENTY-SIX

Favour Can Raise a Voice for You in Your Absence

Acts 5:34-35 (KJV): *Then stood there up one in the council, a Pharisee, named Gamaliel, a doctor of the law, had in reputation among all the people, and commanded to put the apostles forth a little space; And said unto them, Ye men of Israel, take heed to yourselves what ye intend to do as touching these men.*

In Acts 5, the disciples were arrested and brought before the council, but the Lord raised a voice for them in the person of Gamaliel, who persuaded the council to let the disciples alone. When someone you did not send starts defending your course, it is because divine favour is set into motion for your sake.

When a person finds favour with God in his absence, a voice will be raised to defend and fight his course. It is impossible for you to be everywhere defending yourself, but favour can do it for you.

Are you concerned that an important decision will be made about you in your absence? Fear not, but ask God for favour so that a voice can be raised for you in your absence.

With favour, the Lord can raise for you an agent who will speak well of you in places that matter. Such an agent will defend you into victory because, for your sake, the good hand of God will be upon him. Be assured that whenever God raises a voice for you, nobody will be able to silence such a voice. God can raise for you a wise, intelligent, and competent influencer that everyone will hearken to his voice. Such an agent can rally support for you in places where your case is being discussed.

The Lord can raise an agent who will bring you into the limelight through his voice so that you will enjoy favourable decisions from those who don't know you. With divine favour, there are people who God can raise for you to advertise your potential to people who matter. At the place of judgment, favour can raise a voice that will produce favourable judgment for you. The Lord can raise a channel of deliverance for you so that you can escape bondage through a voice assigned by heaven. There is a voice that can connect you to destiny helpers, such that those who don't know you will do you good. Divine favour can do it through a voice you don't know.

Prayer: Father, give me the favour that will raise for me a voice in my absence, in Jesus' name.

CHAPTER TWENTY-SEVEN

Favour Can Make You Come Out Stronger from Difficult Situations

2 Kings 4:1 (KJV): *Now there cried a certain woman of the wives of the sons of the prophets unto Elisha, saying, Thy servant my husband is dead; and thou knowest that thy servant did fear the LORD: and the creditor is come to take unto him my two sons to be bondmen.*

2 Kings 4:7 (KJV): *Then she came and told the man of God. And he said, Go, sell the oil, and pay thy debt, and live thou and thy children of the rest.*

When someone finds favour in his difficult situation, such a situation will turn out to be a blessing as the person comes out far better than he was before he entered that situation.

In 2 Kings 4:1-7, a widow has a debt to settle, and by the end of the story, she not only settles the debt but has more than enough for herself and her children to live on.

Her difficult situation turned out to be a blessing, and she came out stronger from it.

Are you going through a difficult situation that is probably degrading your life? Fear not, because with divine favour, you will emerge stronger from that situation.

The Lord that turned the difficult situation of the widow in 1 Kings 4 into a blessing for her will do the same thing for you, and your difficult situation will turn out to be a blessing to you.

With divine favour at work in your life, every disappointment can be turned into an appointment, and every troubling situation can become a blessing.

When favour is fully at work in your life, the situation devouring you can start enriching you, and your poverty can be changed into prosperity.

With favour, the same place where you face hardship can bring you a better experience and softness. Favour improves things and can make you stronger where you were once in a weak position. With divine favour, the same situation that makes life very difficult for you can be turned around such that you come out richer than before. When you find yourself in a difficult situation, pray to God to grant you favour so that things will turn around and you can emerge stronger and better from that situation.

Prayer: Father, give me the favour that will make me come out stronger from every difficult life situation, in Jesus' name.

CHAPTER TWENTY-EIGHT

Favour Can Take You out of Impossible Pits

Genesis 37:28 (KJV): *Then there passed by Midianites merchantmen; and they drew and lifted up Joseph out of the pit, and sold Joseph to the Ishmeelites for twenty pieces of silver: and they brought Joseph into Egypt.*

The brethren of Joseph threw him inside a pit. The pit was so deep that Joseph couldn't come out of it by himself. There was nothing Joseph could do to help himself out of this terrible and deep pit. The favour of God protected Joseph while inside the pit and took him out of it. It was not the enemies' goodwill that brought Joseph out of this pit but divine favour. With divine favour, the same enemies that put Joseph inside the pit brought him out of it.

Are you inside a terrible and difficult pit? Are you in a problem so terrible that you can't do anything to help yourself out of it? If you answer yes to those questions, fear not. Instead of being afraid, ask God, who took Joseph out of the impossible pit, to come and do the same for you.

When you walk in favour, those who do you evil can willingly reverse the evil work they did against you. When you find yourself in a problem whereby you are totally helpless to bring yourself out of it, cry to God for favour.

The Lord can draw you out of any pit of trouble, irrespective of how deep and terrible it may appear. The problem is that hiding you from a human helper can't hide you from God. The helpless situation making you invisible to helpers can't do the same with God. Divine favour can break any power hiding you from helpers and raise those that will draw you out of the pit of the wicked.

With divine favour, your little cry for help will be heard by able helpers who will draw you out of the pit of the wicked. Favour makes your helpers hear and hearken to your cry for help. Divine favour removes every high thing hiding you from your helper. Whatever represents an invisible mountain hindering your removal from any pit can be disgraced by divine favour. No evil hand or dark shadow can impede the escape of a person who carries divine favour from any pit of the wicked. Divine favour can make the light of God shine on you so that your helpers can identify you for deliverance.

With the favour of God, you will come out of every dry place, and any wall the enemy has built roundabout you to keep you inside the pit will be destroyed. The Lord, higher than any high or deep pit, will rescue you because you carry favour.

Prayer: Father, give me the favour that will take me out of any impossible pit, in Jesus' name.

CHAPTER TWENTY-NINE

Favour Can Dissolve Threats Meant to Come to Pass Against Your Life

Exodus 15:9-10 (KJV): *The enemy said, I will pursue, I will overtake, I will divide the spoil; my lust shall be satisfied upon them; I will draw my sword, my hand shall destroy them. Thou didst blow with thy wind, the sea covered them: they sank as lead in the mighty waters.*

Sometimes, the capability of the person who threatens you determines how seriously you will take such a threat. There are certain people that you should never take as unimportant when they issue threats against your life. This is because you know they can carry out their threats.

In Exodus 15:9-10, King Pharaoh threatened Israel, but God, who is greater than the greatest, dissolved all his threats, and none came to pass. Truly, King Pharaoh had the capacity to carry out all his threats, but divine favour on Israel made God arise against him such that none of his threats came to pass.

Is your life facing any threat from anybody or situation? Are you afraid of any threats because you know that the person or situation threatening you has all the capacity to carry it out? Instead of being afraid, you should ask God to send you a favour that will dissolve every threat from any capable enemy. With divine favour on you, the Lord can make all the threats issued against you come to nought. Threats against your destiny, job, family, or anything concerning you by any powerful enemy will come to nothing because divine favour is upon you. Similarly, any threat issued against your health by any deadly and killing sickness or threats issued against you by fear or hardship will come to nothing because divine favour is upon you. The threat that came to pass against someone you know will not come to pass against you because you carry divine favour. With divine favour upon your life, the Lord will make every destruction prepared for your life by the enemy come to nothing. This is because divine favour guarantees your security, and whoever is pursuing your life, the Lord will overthrow them. You will rejoice over what the enemy has prepared to make you weep. When you face credible threats, fear not because divine favour upon your life will make the Lord arise for your sake against every threat issued against your life.

Prayer: Father, give me the favour that will dissolve every threat that is supposed to come to pass against me, in Jesus' name.

CHAPTER THIRTY

Favour Can Bring You Life

Psalm 30:5 (KJV): *For his anger endureth but a moment; in his favour is life: weeping may endure for a night, but joy cometh in the morning.*

According to the above Bible verse, divine favour brings life. Life is the opposite of death. When someone walks in divine favour, every good thing that has died can come back to life while things that are alive are preserved.

Favour promotes well-being and hinders everything that can kill.

Are you under the threat of death? Has any good thing that belonged to you about to die? Instead of staying in sorrow, you should ask God for divine favour that brings life.

When a person is under the influence of divine favour, what the enemy has marked to die will live, and what the enemy has killed can resurrect.

There is life in divine favour. Furthermore, where there is life, there will be growth because good things don't die under the influence of the favour of God. Where there is life, there will be promotion because stagnancy can't survive in the presence of divine favour. The kind of life divine favour brings also eliminates sickness and diseases that are the agents of death. If you are under the threat of sickness and diseases, ask God for divine favour to eliminate them from your life. When someone is under divine favour, every good thing he puts his hand on will thrive because death is eliminated with divine favour. With divine favour, there is progress and speed because stagnancy is removed. With divine favour, there is joy and peace because sorrow and mourning that work with death are sent far away. Divine favour brings life that guarantees your well-being and keeps you in good health.

Similarly, divine favour brings life that guarantees the abundance of good things. With the favour of God on you, there will be an overflow of blessings as evidence of the abundant life divine favour brings. Every attack from agents of death against your life is terminated because you are walking in divine favour. No power of hell can waste your life, good effort, or any of your possessions because divine favour is on you. Henceforth, be assured that life is yours because you carry divine favour.

Prayer: Father, give me the favour that brings life to make all that belongs to me live, in Jesus' name.

CHAPTER THIRTY-ONE

Favour Can Fast-Forward Your Journey

1 Kings 18:46 (KJV): *and the hand of the lord was on Elijah; and he girded up his loins, and ran before Ahab to the entrance of Jezreel.*

In the story above, the journey that was supposed to take Elijah many hours took him a few minutes—he finished the journey quickly ahead of time.

This was made possible because God's hand came on him to fast-forward his journey. It should be noted that Elijah did not pray for the hand of God to come on him when he was in this situation, but God's favour did it for him.

When a man receives favour from God, the journey that is supposed to take him many years to complete could take him a few months because God fast-forwards his journey. When a man walks in divine favour, he will enjoy the divine intervention he did not ask God for because God's favour is at work in his life.

Are you facing delays or concerned that time is working against you in certain areas of your life? Are you concerned that time is going on, yet you have not achieved much in some areas of your life? Instead of becoming anxious, it is better to ask God for divine favour to fast-forward your situation and give you supernatural accelerated promotion in your endeavours.

Divine favour can fast-forward your promotion such that every force keeping you in one position is broken. With divine favour, the good decisions that should be made concerning your promotion can be made quickly without any delay. Similarly, divine favour can fast-forward your healing such that healing that is supposed to take place gradually can happen fast.

With divine favour, your breakthrough can be fast-tracked, and every obstacle delaying your good testimonies can be removed. Divine favour can fast-track your perfection so that everything starts working together for your good quickly. When you walk in divine favour, your turning can be accelerated so that every necessary change your situations require is done without delay. Divine favour can expedite your victory, harvest, and the delivery of answers to your prayers. With divine favour, wasters, troublers, and enemies of your good expectations are removed from your situation. When you need speed, cry to God for divine favour.

Prayer: Father, give me the favour that will expedite my journey and quicken into manifestations all my pending good testimonies, in Jesus' name.

CHAPTER THIRTY-TWO

Favour Can Give You Victory over the Secret Plot of the Enemy

2 Kings 6:8-9 (KJV): *Then the king of Syria warred against Israel, and took counsel with his servants, saying, In such and such a place shall be my camp. And the man of God sent unto the king of Israel, saying, Beware that thou pass not such a place; for thither the Syrians are come down.*

It is practically impossible for you to know everything concerning you, especially things going on behind you. However, when you find favour with God, He gives you victory over every secret agenda of the enemy against you. You will begin to walk in victory over the battle you don't know.

In 2 Kings 6:8-9, the king of Israel had no clue that the king of Syria was plotting against him, but because of divine favour, the enemy's secret plot was exposed to the king of Israel. The king of Syria later became worried when he saw that all his secret plots against the king of Israel did not work.

Similarly, in your life, when you find favour with God, you will begin to gain access to the secret agenda of the wicked against you and start walking in victory against the plot of the enemy.

Are you afraid that some people may be plotting evil against you behind your back? Fear not about any secret plot of the wicked against you. Instead, ask God for divine favour to defend you. With divine favour on you, the Lord can overthrow every sudden attack the enemy is plotting against you. For a person walking in divine favour, the Lord will bring frustration to those chasing his life for evil. There is no evil chaser that can succeed against you because divine favour will defend you. Even those working for your enemies against you will fail because you carry God's favour upon your life. Wherever the wicked gather against you, divine favour will speak for you and speak against the enemies. Divine favour gives assurance of victory against any secret plot of the wicked. There is no wickedness formed against you that will prosper because you are a child of divine favour. The Lord is more than willing to war against those who war against you, irrespective of their location. Whoever gathers in a secret place against you will be scattered, and their evil camp will be brought to nothing. The Lord will lighten every dark area of your life and expose every secret plot of your enemies. The Lord will supervise all your goings and give you victory over every device of the enemy.

Prayer: Father, give me the favour that will give me victory over every secret plot of the enemy against me, in Jesus' name.

CHAPTER THIRTY-THREE

Favour Can Separate You from General Problems

2 Kings 8:1-2 (KJV): *Then spake Elisha unto the woman, whose son he had restored to life, saying, Arise, and go thou and thine household, and sojourn wheresoever thou canst sojourn: for the LORD hath called for a famine; and it shall also come upon the land seven years. And the woman arose, and did after the saying of the man of God: and she went with her household, and sojourned in the land of the Philistines seven years.*

In the above Bible verses, without any prior knowledge about the coming famine, the woman in the above story was told to relocate to another land because the famine was coming. The woman enjoyed an unusual favour that gave her a way to escape from coming trouble. She moved away from the land before the days of evil arrived.

Divine favour can separate you from general problems that will come against everyone around you. It is possible not to partake in the sorrow and mourning that will come to everyone around you. It is possible to be totally separated from any pandemic. With divine favour, immunity against any evil is available.

Are you worrying about any pandemic? Are you afraid that you may suffer from the evil that befalls those around you? Fear not, but ask God for divine favour to grant you immunity and separate you from every evil that will befall those around you. With divine favour, you will only hear or see the evil that befalls the world, but it shall not come near you. With His favour, the Lord can make your case different so that you will not partake in every sorrow and mourning that will come to those around you. It is possible for you not to partake in problems that run in your bloodline because you find favour with God. It is possible for you to enjoy special immunity against poverty and hardship befalling those around you. It is possible for you to say there is a lifting up when others are saying casting down is the order of the day. It is possible for you to enjoy good health during a season that is causing other people sickness. It is possible for you to make a profit from things that cause other people losses. Do not expect or connect yourself to any evil that befalls the world; instead, cry to God for His favour to separate you from every evil befalling the world.

Prayer: Father, give me the favour that will separate me and my home from problems that befall the world, in Jesus' name.

CHAPTER THIRTY-FOUR

Favour Can Grant You an Upgrade at No Cost

2 Samuel 9:6-7 (KJV): *Now when Mephibosheth, the son of Jonathan, the son of Saul, was come unto David, he fell on his face, and did reverence. And David said, Mephibosheth. And he answered, Behold thy servant! And David said unto him, Fear not: for I will surely shew thee kindness for Jonathan thy father's sake, and will restore thee all the land of Saul thy father; and thou shalt eat bread at my table continually.*

An upgrade means to increase or lift up the grade, such as an increase in the standard or quality of living. God is really interested in upgrading you so that the quality or standard of your life increases.

In 2 Samuel 9:6-7, Mephibosheth was upgraded by King David, and he moved him from being a common man to an important person who would be eating and dining at the same table with the king of the land. It is important to state that this kind of upgrading came to Mephibosheth at no cost. There was nothing he did to qualify for such betterment. Favour did it for him. With divine favour, your life can be far better than it is now. It is possible for you to move from glory to glory and blessing to blessing. Are you tired of staying at the lowest level of the ladder of destiny? Do you need upgrading in certain areas of your life? Do you desire to rise in your career, ministry, dreams, and visions? Truly, you may not be able to achieve this for yourself, but divine favour is available for you as a child of God. With divine favour, you can experience upgrading in any area of your life as you desire. You don't need to accept it as your cross—a life void of meaningful progress. With divine favour, you can access the better and more treasurable things of this world at no cost—divine favour settles the cost for you. Divine favour can grant you an upgrade in fruitfulness, whereby you have more space to be more fruitful in all that you do. You can enjoy an upgrade in social status whereby you have more influence on situations around you, in which your word becomes a law everyone obeys. With divine favour, you can have an upgrade in access to resources, whereby every good thing you need for your life comes to you in greater quantity. You can be upgraded in speed, whereby the time you spend completing any project is reduced to achieve more good things within the shortest time. Divine favour makes upgrade possible.

Prayer: Father, give me the favour that will grant me an upgrade in every facet of life, in Jesus' name.

CHAPTER THIRTY-FIVE

Favour Can Move You from One Level of Favour to Another

Genesis 39:21 (KJV): *But the LORD was with Joseph, and shewed him mercy, and gave him favour in the sight of the keeper of the prison.*

The Lord's presence was with Joseph, and he was given wherever he went. Joseph experienced favour galore because the Lord was with him.

In his journey of destiny, Joseph found favour with God, which gave him favour with Potiphar when he was a servant in his house. This divine favour also gave Joseph favour with the keeper of the prison. After prison, King Pharaoh showed favour to Joseph, and later, the whole of Egypt started to show favour to Joseph. The divine favour Joseph enjoyed was not localised but general because wherever he went, he enjoyed favour from everyone who made contact with him. Joseph enjoyed favour from every system or organisation he came across in Egypt. All things and all people showed favour to Joseph.

Are you afraid that the favour you enjoy in a place may end when restructuring takes place? Are you fearful that favour may cease in your life due to a change of location? Fear not; as long as God's presence is with you wherever you go, you will enjoy favour. The operation of divine favour is not localised but general. God is a God of all flesh, and when you find favour with Him, He makes all flesh to show you favour. The earth is of the Lord and the fulness therein. Therefore, the Lord is able to make all things, both tangible and intangible, show you favour, irrespective of location. God rules over all things; therefore, He can make every organisation or system you come in contact with show you favour. Wherever you go, the eyes of the Lord are on you to give you favour.

Fear not when there is a change around you because regardless of who comes to be in charge, God can give you favour with the person.

Whatever alteration occurs in the system or organisation where you function, God can give you favour with them. Things may change, but the Lord who gives favour changes not.

Therefore, face the future with hope and good expectations that the Lord who cared for you now will take good care of you tomorrow. Divine favour can follow you wherever you go and make all things serve you well. In all changes, fear not, for the Lord is with you and will always give you favour.

Prayer: Father, give me the favour that will take me from favour to favour, in Jesus' name.

CHAPTER THIRTY-SIX

Favour Can Cause Pleasant Coincidences for You

2 Kings 8:4-6 (KJV): *And the king talked with Gehazi the servant of the man of God, saying, Tell me, I pray thee, all the great things that Elisha hath done. And it came to pass, as he was telling the king how he had restored a dead body to life, that, behold, the woman, whose son he had restored to life, cried to the king for her house and for her land. And Gehazi said, My lord, O king, this is the woman, and this is her son, whom Elisha restored to life. And when the king asked the woman, she told him. So the king appointed unto her a certain officer, saying, Restore all that was hers, and all the fruits of the field since the day that she left the land, even until now.*

In the above Bible story, a woman who wanted to recover the land taken from her during her departure from the land entered the king's palace to lodge her case. This woman entered the palace while Gehazi was discussing her matter with the king. This pleasant coincidence made the case of the woman easy, and she was able to find favour with the king.

When a person walks in divine favour, there will be pleasant coincidences that will bring him blessings. Favour prepares a good ground for you before you arrive at places that matter.

Will you appear before any panels or organisations dealing with your matter? Fear not, because divine favour is able to arrange pleasant coincidences for you to advance your matter.

When a person finds favour with God, the Lord can send favour ahead of him to wherever the person will go for a deal. Pleasant coincidences enable you to easily receive what other people struggle to obtain.

With pleasant coincidences, the Lord may arrange approval concerning your case without your effort. Divine favour can arrange situations that bring you effortless approval concerning your cases, and you will receive acceptance on a platter of gold. Divine favour will put you in the right place at the right time because your steps are divinely arranged and ordered. As a child of favour, the Lord orders your steps to places of restoration as you enjoy guidance from heaven. When there is a need for someone to speak and defend you in a place, divine favour can raise a voice that will create a positive influence for your sake. Situations will begin to work together for your sake because divine favour is at work in your life.

Due to God's favour upon your life, the hearts of many people can be prepared simultaneously for your benefits over situations that matter to you. When favour is at work in your life, people who used to disagree can suddenly come together to promote your course. In some situations, divine favour arranges it in such a way that when you seek a job, a certain organisation will advertise vacancies that will suit you. It is a pleasant coincidence arranged by favour for your sake.

Prayer: Father, give me a favour that will cause pleasant coincidences for my sake in places that matter, in Jesus' name.

CHAPTER THIRTY-SEVEN

Favour Can Cause Good Things to Seek for You

1 Kings 10:1-2 (KJV): *And when the queen of Sheba heard of the fame of Solomon concerning the name of the LORD, she came to prove him with hard questions. And she came to Jerusalem with a very great train, with camels that bare spices, and very much gold, and precious stones: and when she was come to Solomon, she communed with him of all that was in her heart.*

When a person is walking in favour, good people begin to seek him out to bless him with their substances.

In 1 Kings 10:1-2, Queen Sheba came to King Solomon to bless him. Divine favour on Solomon moved her to travel a long distance to come and bless Solomon.

Are you struggling with lack and poverty? The blessings you need are in another man's hand, and only divine favour can bring it to you.

When a person finds favour with God, those God has entrusted blessings into their hands will arise to seek out that person and deliver those blessings to them. It is divine favour that will make a fellow human being so interested in your well-being that he is ready to bless you in advance for your standard of living. There is nothing you need in life that is not in the hands of somebody somewhere, but it is divine favour that will arrange how those blessings can be transferred to you. With divine favour, promotion can start seeking for you such that your employers will invite you for a discussion to give you the promotion you did not even seek. With divine favour, precious things of life can start seeking you. Divine favour can raise up someone to come to you and bless you. With divine favour, it is possible for you to enjoy gifts you did not ask for, the harvest you did not plant, and treasures you did not search for. Divine favour can give you victory without a battle because someone else has fought the battle for you. Divine favour can bring you houses you did not build because the builder gave you what he has built over time. With divine favour, your life can be flooded with pleasant things you did not invite or seek for. When God decides to favour you, life becomes easier than you can imagine. When it seems you are in a difficult situation, never lose hope because, without your effort, good things can seek you wherever life puts you.

Prayer: Father, give me the favour that will make good things seek for me, in Jesus' name.

CHAPTER THIRTY-EIGHT

Favour Can Make Your Destiny Helpers That Had Forgotten You Remember You

Genesis 40:23 (KJV): *Yet did not the chief butler remember Joseph, but forgat him.*

In the above Bible verse, the chief butler forgot to introduce Joseph's case to the king, but in Genesis 41:9-12, he eventually did.

When favour is at work in your life, those who had forgotten about helping you will start remembering you.

Are you feeling forgotten in life? Does it seem as if nobody cares to help you? Fear not, but cry out to God for favour, because when favour is set into motion on your behalf, all who carry your blessings and had forgotten you will be quickened to come and bless you.

When divine favour is at work in your life, those that heaven has chosen to be your destiny helpers will start to remember you. Favour will not allow those that heaven has ordained to help you rest, even though the enemy has made them forget you. Many people may keep quiet concerning your case, but divine favour will not. The devil can make competent helpers not notice you in your struggle, but divine favour will not. It is a matter of time—all the destiny helpers the devil has made to forget you will wake up from their slumber to help you.

Any organisation that has forgotten to respond favourably to your application will wake up and become restless until they attend to your case. Whoever has genuinely forgotten to attend to your matter will not rest until he deals with your case successfully.

With divine favour, all those who had forgotten to release your blessings in their custody will wake up to release your ordained blessings in their hands. Divine favour will arrest whoever heaven has chosen to promote your deliverance in order to assist you. When favour is at work in your life, you can't be forgotten for a long time by your destiny helpers.

Prayer: Father, give me the favour that will make my destiny helpers remember me, in Jesus' name.

CHAPTER THIRTY-NINE

Favour Can Bring You Unceasing Help

1 Chronicles 12:22 (KJV): *For at that time day by day there came to David to help him, until it was a great host, like the host of God.*

The above Bible verse says that day by day, people came to help David. Help kept coming to him, and he never lacked help.

When someone walks in divine favour, he will never lack help because wherever he turns, there will always be people waiting to help him. Such a person experiences unceasing help. With divine favour, another door has already been opened before one door of support closes. Similarly, with divine favour, things get better and better in terms of help. Favour takes you from one better help to another better help.

Are you becoming concerned that the present door of help you are enjoying may close? Are you not satisfied with the support you receive from certain places? If you can believe it, the Lord can grant you unceasing help by opening doors of support that will never close.

With divine favour, the Lord is willing to send you help that you have not asked for—help that is beyond your prayer request. God can send you help that will satisfy your present and future needs.

Divine favour can move so mightily in your life that before your needs for help arise, help is already waiting. This means that you will not need to wait in anticipation for help because help has come ahead of the needs.

There is help that can outweigh your need for help. There is a help that can terminate your thirst for help and sort you out permanently. There is help that ends all your struggles. God can give you such help because you are highly favoured. God can make help to start pursuing you such that wherever you go, help is waiting for you. Which areas of life do you need help with, and how many types of help do you need? With divine favour, help that breeds more help is available. God is able to open multiple doors of help for you, ensuring that you will never lack assistance, no matter how much help you need. When you face many needs for help, fear not, but ask God for it, and your joy will overflow.

Prayer: Father, give me the favour that will grant me unceasing help, in Jesus' name.

CHAPTER FORTY

Favour Can Cut Off All the Enemies That Rise Against You

2 Samuel 7:8-9 (KJV): *Now therefore so shalt thou say unto my servant David, Thus saith the LORD of hosts, I took thee from the sheepcote, from following the sheep, to be ruler over my people, over Israel: And I was with thee whithersoever thou wentest, and have cut off all thine enemies out of thy sight, and have made thee a great name, like unto the name of the great men that are in the earth.*

In the above Bible verses, God showed David favour by cutting off all his enemies from his ways. David's prayer or righteousness did not cause God to act in this way; rather, it was God's favour.

When you find favour with God, He will intentionally remove all those making your life difficult from your ways. Enemies are forces that seek to hinder, antagonise, or cause you harm. Such forces could be humans or spiritual beings.

Are you under the attack of enemies such as human enemies or demonic enemies? Fear not, because divine favour can make God raise an attack against all your attackers.

With divine favour on your life, God can remove from your way every category of enemy rising against your life wherever they have been planted.

As a child of favour, the Lord can cut off from your way enemies planted at the place of your work to attack you. God will remove those seeking your hurt at work from your way.

Divine favour can overthrow household enemies hired against you so that they are all cut off from your way.

As a child of favour, all your bosses or seniors, especially at your place of work, who have become your enemies, will be removed from your way as the Lord cut them off from your path. All those chasing you for evil will soon be worn out because divine favour will defend you against them.

Similarly, all those who hate you because you are above them will be desolate because divine favour will fight for you. Enemies pretending to be your friends will not succeed against you because you are under the cover of divine favour.

Prayer: Father, give me the favour that will cut off all the enemies standing against me, in any place, in Jesus' name.

Prayers on Divine Favour

Father, I thank you for making me a child of divine favour. Blessed be your name.

Father, release on me today favour that sets the captive free, in Jesus' name.

Father, release on me today favour that turns impossibility to possibility, in Jesus' name.

Father, release on me today favour that will make me triumph over my strong enemy, in Jesus' name.

Father, I declare that because I am highly favoured; therefore, I shall never suffer rejection, in Jesus' name.

Father, in your favour, turn all my mistakes into miracles for me, in Jesus' name.

Father, in your favour, remove from me every battle I have ignorantly invited into my life, in Jesus' name.

Father, let your favour separate me from every collective affliction, in Jesus' name.

Father, release on me today favour that will make me rise to the level beyond my natural ability, in Jesus' name.

Father, in your favour, help me marvellously in all I do, in Jesus' name.

Father, in your favour, let every good thing start seeking for me, in Jesus' name.

Father, you are the Almighty, let your favour make me stronger than all my enemies, in Jesus' name.

Father, from today, let your favour make me noticeable to people that matter, in Jesus' name.

Father, let your favour take me out of darkness into the limelight, in Jesus' name.

Father, in your favour, let every dominion of the power of darkness over my life be broken today, in Jesus' name.

Father, let your favour bring me to the place where I will shine for you, in Jesus' name.

Father, in your favour, let my life please you in all my days, in Jesus' name.

Father, let your favour make me stand out among the crowd, in Jesus' name.

Father, from today, let your favour begin to announce my gifting to the world, in Jesus' name.

Father, in your favour, grant me the kind of achievements that nobody has ever recorded in my generation, in Jesus' name.

Father, let your favour grant me the opportunity to show and develop my potential, in Jesus' name.

Father, let your favour bring me before great men, in Jesus' name.

Father, in your favour, make me a solution carrier to the world, in Jesus' name.

Father, in your favour, let all my destiny helpers begin to seek for me, in Jesus' name.

Father, let your favour take me to places where my giftings will be rewarded, in Jesus' name.

Father, let your favour turn my depreciation to appreciation, in Jesus' name.

Father, let your favour make my rising speedy, in Jesus' name.

Father, in your favour, let the power that suppresses the destiny of those in my bloodline fail over my life, in Jesus' name.

Father, in your favour, in all my days, make me undefeatable in destiny, in Jesus' name.

Father, in your favour, release on me the grace of an achiever, in Jesus' name.

Father, in your favour, wherever I go, let people willingly submit to me and serve me, in Jesus' name.

Father, in your favour, advertise yourself in my life as a lifter of my head, in Jesus' name.

Father, let your favour make me untouchable to every evil troubling the world, in Jesus' name.

Father, in your favour, grant me deliverance nobody has ever received in my bloodline, in Jesus' name.

Father, let your favour make me leap over every wall separating me from my good testimonies, in Jesus' name.

Father, wherever my name is mentioned, let your favour always answer for me in Jesus' name.

Father, in your favour, advertise my strength to frighten all my enemies to submission, in Jesus' name.

Father, in your favour, mobilise every created thing to work against all my enemies for my sake, in Jesus' name.

Father, in your favour, supply me with every resource I need to always walk in victory, in Jesus' name.

Father, wherever the enemy has arranged disfavour for me, let your favour defend me, in Jesus' name.

Father, in your favour, forces that hinder those in my bloodline, let them fail in my life, in Jesus' name.

Father, in your favour, separate me from the generational evil pattern, in Jesus' name.

Father, in your favour, arise and trouble all my troublers, in Jesus' name.

Father, in your favour, order my steps to victory in all my battles, in Jesus' name.

Father, let your favour drive everything called sickness and disease of Egypt far away from me in all my days, in Jesus' name.

Father, in your favour, let all things always work together for my good, in Jesus' name.

Father, in your favour, send your angels to help me till I win all my battles, in Jesus' name.

Father, where people record failure, let your favour grant me success in Jesus' name.

Father, in your favour, turn all my enemies into friends, in Jesus' name.

Father, in your favour, whatever enemy sent to harm me, let it bless me, in Jesus' name.

Father, in your favour, arise and make the way of every evil chaser assigned against me difficult, in Jesus' name.

Father, in your favour, let people who matter come together for my lifting, in Jesus' name.

Father, in your favour, let every armour and instrument of war the enemy prepared against me fail, in Jesus' name.

Father, in your favour, I declare prophetically that only your counsel will stand in all that concerns me, in Jesus' name.

Father, in your favour, I declare prophetically that I shall always walk in divine wisdom, in Jesus' name.

Father, in your favour, I declare prophetically that no matter how fast my competitors run, they will always find me in front, in Jesus' name.

Father, in your favour, I declare prophetically that I shall do excellently in all my endeavours, in Jesus' name.

Father, in your favour, I declare prophetically that I shall always find direction, for you will show me the way to go in all my situations, in Jesus' name.

Father, in your favour, I declare prophetically that there will always be divine preservation over all that is mine, in Jesus' name.

Father, by your favour, I prophetically declare a divine turnaround in every injustice I have suffered, in Jesus' name.

Father, in your favour, I declare prophetically that your mighty hand will move me from weakness to strength and from curses to blessings, in Jesus' name.

Father, in your favour, I declare prophetically that what has been working against me shall start to work for me, in Jesus' name.

Father, in your favour, I declare prophetically that all those who witnessed my loss will also witness my gain, in Jesus' name.

Father, in your favour, I declare prophetically that every bad news the enemy has prepared for me shall be turned into good news, in Jesus' name.

Father, let your favour turn me into a prosperous person in every facet of life, in Jesus' name.

Father, let your favour take me to a height beyond the reach of my natural ability, in Jesus' name.

Father, let your favour turn my life from a magnet to success, in Jesus' name.

Father, let your favour make it work for me, what is not working for other people, in Jesus' name.

Father, in all my days, when other people are saying casting down, let your favour make me say lifting up, in Jesus' name.

Father, let your favour raise a voice for me in places that matter, in Jesus' name.

Father, in your favour, cause favourable shaking that will replace every hater the devil has brought into my life with those who will genuinely love me, in Jesus' name.

Father, let your favour turn the place of my affliction to that of blessings for me, in Jesus's name.

Father, let your favour give me a good harvest far greater than my good sowing, in Jesus' name.

Father, let your favour make a space for me in every place where I operate, in Jesus' name.

Father, let your favour return to sender, every evil arrow the enemy directed at any area of my life, in Jesus' name.

Father, in your favour, bless me and make me a blessing to nations, in Jesus' name.

Father, in your favour and for my sake, devour every devourer assigned against my life, in Jesus' name.

Father, let your favour make my voice be heard in every area of life where the enemy has made me voiceless, in Jesus' name.

Father, let your favour make me unbreakable to forces that break people of the world, in Jesus' name.

Father, let your favour silence every silencer assigned against my life, in Jesus' name.

Father, in your favour, lead me away from the pit the wicked dug for me, in Jesus' name.

Father, let your favour recover for me with dividends, every good thing I had lost to the enemy, in Jesus' name.

Father, let your favour grant me access to the treasures in dark places, in Jesus' name.

Father, let your favour bring me to places where my divine allocations are waiting for me, in Jesus' name.

Father, in your favour, let my rising be easy, in Jesus' name.

Father, let your favour enlarge me in places where I have been made small, in Jesus' name.

Father, let your favour turn my place of barrenness into the place of fruitfulness, in Jesus's name.

Father, let your favour make me bold against things that make me afraid, in Jesus' name.

Father, let your favour grant me light in every dark area of my life, in Jesus' name.

Father, let your favour open multiple doors of opportunities to me in many places, in Jesus' name.

Father, in your favour, move out of my way every stubborn mountain standing before me, in Jesus' name.

Father, in your favour, let me walk in dominion over whatever has been dominating me, in Jesus' name.

Father, for my sake, let your favour cause a rearrangement of situations in places that matter, in Jesus' name.

Father, before the sun rises tomorrow, let your favour open for me every good door the enemy has closed against me, in Jesus' name.

Father, in your favour, the fire that burns people of the world shall not burn me, in Jesus' name.

Father, I declare and decree that your favour shall make every benevolent hand the enemy has made to close against me open unto me, in Jesus' name.

Father, I declare and decree that your favour will end the reign of ungodly delay in every affair of my life, in Jesus' name.

Father, I declare and decree that your favour will make heaven always honour my voice, in Jesus' name.

Father, I declare and decree that I shall dwell in the abundance of your provisions all the days of my life, in Jesus' name.

Father, I declare and decree that in all my days, I shall always find favour with God and all men, in Jesus' name.

Father, let your favour disgrace every opposition standing against my desires in all places, in Jesus' name.

Father, let your favour make all my journeys peaceful and fruitful, in Jesus' name.

Father, in your favour, send far away from me the sons of wickedness, in Jesus' name.

Father, let your favour enforce wellness in all that concerns me, in Jesus' name.

Father, in your favour, send me help beyond the understanding of the human mind, in Jesus' name.

Father, send me the favour that breaks in my life every physical, spiritual, and human barrier, in Jesus' name.

Father, send me the favour that will break the record of divine assistance in my life, assistance I have not received before, in Jesus' name.

Father, send me the favour that will make my enemies become friends such that all those who oppose me will surrender in Jesus' name.

Father, send me the favour that will aid me in discovering places of hidden treasures, in Jesus' name.

Father, send me the favour that will raise an army of helpers for me, in Jesus' name.

Father, because I am highly favoured, I decree that henceforth, wherever I turn, I will always find suitable helpers, in Jesus' name.

Father, in your favour, anoint me with fresh and great ideas that will transform my life, in Jesus' name.

Father, send me the favour that will make me strong spiritually, financially, mentally, materially, and in every facet of life, in Jesus' name.

Father, send me the favour that will qualify me for help that brings restoration, in Jesus' name.

Father, send me the favour that will relocate all my oppressors far away from me, in Jesus' name.

Father, in your favour, lift all my burdens, in Jesus' name.

Father, in your favour, bring a permanent end to all my sufferings, in Jesus' name.

Father, in your favour, let every disagreement the devil has caused among those handling my case be resolved today for my sake, in Jesus' name.

Father, in your favour, let all those sitting on my inheritance be unseated today, in Jesus' name.

Father, send me the favour that will put to shame all those that the devil has assigned to undermine my authority, where you had planted me, in Jesus' name.

Father, let your favour fight for me such that your hand will always be against all those against me, in Jesus' name.

Father, in your favour, let every negative wind blowing in my place of operation never touch me, in Jesus' name.

Father, in your favour, whoever the devil wants to raise to replace me where you had planted me, let them fail in their mission, in Jesus' name.

Father, in your favour, every household the enemy devil has hired against me, cut them off from my way from today, in Jesus' name.

Father, in your favour, let all the haters of my glory be silent in darkness, in Jesus' name.

Father, let your favour arise for me and cut off all who have made themselves my enemies, in Jesus' name.

Father, in your favour, guide me to never depend on the wrong people, in Jesus' name.

Father, let your favour arise for me and defend me against enemies without a cause, ungrateful and envious enemies, in Jesus' name.

Father, in your favour, let every wall on my way fall flat, in Jesus' name.

Father, in your favour, carry me and make all my journeys effortless, in Jesus' name.

Father, in your favour, order my steps to my divine destinations in all my endeavours, in Jesus' name.

Father, in your favour, take evil far away from my ways, in Jesus' name.

Father, in your favour, let me operate on your strength in all my undertakings, in Jesus' name.

Father, let your favour connect me to an agent of uncommon restoration of all my lost blessings, in Jesus' name.

Father, in your favour, let every closed heaven over my life be reversed today, in Jesus' name.

Father, let your favour reveal to me the secrets of unstoppable success, in Jesus' name.

Father, let your favour grant me sudden lifting in every area of my life, in Jesus' name.

Father, in your favour, the great things you promised to do in my life, do it without delay, in Jesus' name.

Father, in your favour, quicken your word for my sake in every area of my life, in Jesus' name.

Father, let your favour activate in every area of my life, a royal anointing, in Jesus' name.

Father, let your favour direct me to the carrier of my good news, in Jesus' name.

Father, let your favour make everything work well for me, in Jesus' name.

Father, in your favour, give me unbreakable peace roundabout, in Jesus' name.

Father, in your favour, let my going out and coming in always be pleasant for me, in Jesus' name.

Father, in all my journeys, let your favour always go ahead of me to remove any device the enemy has placed on my way, in Jesus' name.

Father, let your favour make all things cooperate with my destiny, in Jesus' name.

Father, let your favour silence every rebellion fashioned against me in all places, in Jesus' name.

Father, let your favour grant me the quietness I need to succeed in all my endeavours, in Jesus' name.

Father, let your favour turn every delay I have suffered into a more glorious miracle, in Jesus' name.

Father, let your favour turn every ungodly 'no' I have received as an answer into a 'yes' for me, in Jesus' name.

Father, let your favour remove every opposition to the perfection of all that concerns me, in Jesus' name.

Father, let your favour bring into glorious completion all that you have started building in my life, in Jesus' name.

Father, every opposition standing against my justification to obtain a miracle, let your favour remove it, in Jesus' name.

Father, let your favour turn around every agenda of shame the enemy designed against me, in Jesus' name.

Father, if any evil record stands against my destiny in any place, let your favour remove it today for my sake, in Jesus' name.

Father, I am not qualified for the privileges, so let your favour make me qualified for it, in Jesus' name.

Father, let your favour remove every opposition against your compassion in my life today, in Jesus' name.

Father, if there is any power standing against me at the place of my honour, let your favour remove it today, in Jesus' name.

Father, let your favour grant me uncommon influence wherever I go, in Jesus' name.

Father, let your favour make me rule over those who used to rule over me, in Jesus' name.

Father, from today, let your favour turn me into a source of fear to all my fears, in Jesus' name.

Father, every situation that used to disobey my word, let your favour make them obey my word from today, in Jesus' name.

Father, in your favour, break every resistance to my authority, in Jesus' name.

Father, in your favour, let all my arrogant enemies become humble before me, in Jesus' name.

Father, because of your favour towards me, render powerless all those who unfairly exercise authority over me, in Jesus' name.

Father, let your favour make me a better person ten times than all my competitors, in Jesus' name.

Father, because your favour is upon me, let every power pressing down my potential die now, in Jesus' name.

Father, no matter how fast my competitors run, let your favour always place me ahead of them, in Jesus' name.

Father, in your favour, make my ways confusing to all those monitoring my way for evil, in Jesus' name.

Father, let your favour make me laugh at all those who have been laughing at me, in Jesus' name.

Father, let your favour fight for me so that all those who used to make me speechless will become speechless, in Jesus' name.

Father, among my peers, let your favour turn me to wonder, in Jesus' name.

Father, because your favour is upon me, I decree no more shaking in my life, in Jesus' name.

Father, let your favour make me a judge over all who used to judge me, in Jesus' name.

Father, because your favour is upon me, let every flattering tongue hired against me be cut off, in Jesus' name.

Father, let your favour give an unbeliever as a ransom for my life, in Jesus' name.

Father, let your favour turn all my regrets into miracles for me, in Jesus' name.

Father, let your favour lift me up far above the height I am now, in Jesus' name.

Father, because your favour is upon me, I decree that I shall not sorrow as the people of the world sorrow, in Jesus' name.

Father, let your favour turn all my pains to pleasures for me, in Jesus' name.

Father, because your favour is upon me, let all those who derive pleasure in cheating me regret it, in Jesus' name.

Father, in your favour, grant me recovery of all my losses with dividends, in Jesus' name.

Father, because your favour is upon me, arise and attack all my attackers and let none of them escape your sword, in Jesus' name.

Father, because your favour is upon me, let every panic attack and fear assigned against me by the enemy fail, in Jesus' name.

Father, in all my days, let your favour preserve my liberty in all situations, in Jesus' name.

Father, in your favour towards me, let all those competing with me over my promotion withdraw their candidacy, in Jesus' name.

Father, all those whose minds are made up to trouble me, let your favour cause them to change their minds for my sake, in Jesus' name.

Father, if any appeal is longed against my promotion in any place, let your favour withdraw it, in Jesus' name.

Father, any candidate more qualified than me who wants to compete with me over my open door, let your favour upon my life make them step aside for my sake, in Jesus' name.

Father, in your favour, arise and let my competitor move all his supporters to my side, in Jesus' name.

Father, for my sake, arise and let your favour upon my life remove all those sitting on my seat of glory, in Jesus' name.

Father, in your favour, let there be a shaking that will bring down those who need to be brought down for me to be lifted up, in Jesus' name.

Father, wherever evil influencers are working against me, let your favour upon my life make them irrelevant and let them lose their influences for my sake, in Jesus' name.

Father, because your favour is upon my life, arise and cut off any evil hand altering the calendar of my destiny, in Jesus' name.

Father, all those angry with me because of my elevation, let your favour upon my life make them pleased with me, in Jesus' name.

Father, because I am highly favoured, let all those who will not let me enter my destiny become nothing, in Jesus' name.

Father, let your favour upon my life make my rising to the top trouble-free, in Jesus' name.

Father, because your favour is upon me, let every candidate the enemy has prepared to take promotion due to me be sent on an errand for my sake on the day of my promotion, in Jesus' name.

Father, let your favour make my promotion too hot for the enemy to touch, in Jesus' name.

Father, arise and, in your favour, overthrow every barrier that wants to frustrate my destiny, in Jesus' name.

Father, you have made your blessings my inheritance; let your favour make it so in all my days, in Jesus' name.

Father, in your favour, open unto me the door that my limitations can't close, in Jesus' name.

Father, let your favour draw unto me people who will help me become the person you created me to be, in Jesus' name.

Father, let your favour bring me out of the pit that life has put me in, in Jesus' name.

Father, whatever has incapacitated me, let your favour deliver me from it today, in Jesus' name.

Father, whatever that represents miry clay in my life, let your favour take me out of it today, in Jesus' name.

Father, in your favour, let me always walk in divine assurances in all that concerns me, in Jesus' name.

Father, let your favour cause the light that will expose and disgrace darkness in every area of my life to shine into my life now, in Jesus' name.

Father, in your favour, let my testimony always be that the Lord is my strength, in Jesus' name.

Father, let your favour grant me uncommon pardon over every offence and error I might have committed, in Jesus' name.

Father, let your favour grant me mercy denied to others, in Jesus' name.

Father, let your favour open for me the door of blessings closed against others, in Jesus' name.

Father, let your favour cause what works against others to work for me, in Jesus' name.

Father, let your favour make me considered fit where other people are being declared unfit, in Jesus' name.

Father, let your favour make my voice be heard at the place where people are being made voiceless, in Jesus' name.

Father, let your favour make me strong, what weakens other people, in Jesus' name.

Father, let your favour cause to bring me joy what brings others sorrow, in Jesus' name.

Father, let your favour release me from any lawful captivity, in Jesus' name.

Father, let your favour withdraw for me every right I had given to the enemy over my life, in Jesus' name.

Father, let your favour override and cancel every limitation in my life, in Jesus' name.

Father, let your favour take me above the height nobody has ever reached in my family, in Jesus' name.

Father, let your favour supply every provision I need for whatever I lay my hands on, in Jesus' name.

Father, let your favour make me greater and bigger than all those undermining me in any place, in Jesus' name.

Father, let your favour bring me blessings that will overflow beyond my storeroom, in Jesus' name.

Father, I have worked for other people in your favour; let people start working for me in all my days, in Jesus' name.

Father, let your favour turn my life into a magnet that attracts blessings, in Jesus' name.

Father, let your favour turn every temporary opportunity into a permanent opportunity for me, in Jesus' name.

Father, let your favour enlarge every small door of opportunities in my life, in Jesus' name.

Father, whatever the enemy has designed to work against me, let your favour make it work for me, in Jesus' name.

Father, let your favour grant me treasures without measure, pleasure without pressure, and progress without protest, in Jesus' name.

Father, let your favour put me at the centre of positive attraction wherever I go, in Jesus' name.

Father, let your favour connect me to help that can't fail, in Jesus' name.

Father, let your favour connect me to a voice that can't be silenced, in Jesus' name.

Father, let your favour bring my case to a place of favourable settlement for me, in Jesus' name.

Father, let your favour put me in an advantageous position against my enemy, in Jesus' name.

Father, let your favour make me prevail against enemies stronger than me, in Jesus' name.

Father, let your favour make me say lifting up when other people are saying casting down, in Jesus' name.

Father, let your favour open for me a door that no man can shut, in Jesus' name.

Father, let your favour take me from trauma to triumph in every area of my life, in Jesus' name.

Father, let your favour turn every disorder in my life to order, in Jesus' name.

Father, in your favour, gather for me all that the enemy has scattered in my life, in Jesus' name.

Father, every situation the enemy has designed to cause me mourning, let your favour turn it into dancing for me, in Jesus' name.

Father, every situation the enemy has designed to cause me stress, let your favour turn it into relief, in Jesus' name.

Father, the joy that will make my enemy weep, let your favour grant me today, in Jesus' name.

Father, every situation the enemy has designed to cause me confusion, let your favour make it give me direction, in Jesus' name.

Father, in your favour, what the enemy has made sick in my life, let it regain health today, in Jesus' name.

Father, every situation the enemy has designed to upset me, let your favour make it to calm me down, in Jesus' name.

Father, in your goodness, satisfy me with favour in all my days, in Jesus' name.

Father, let your favour cause goodness and mercy to pursue me in all my days, in Jesus' name.

Father, let your favour make me a candidate for the fullness of joy, in Jesus' name.

Father, for every bad report written concerning me in any place, let your favour turn it into a good report, in Jesus' name.

Father, let your favour make life easy for me in all my days, in Jesus' name.

Father, in your favour, what others pay a heavy price to obtain, let me receive it free of charge, in Jesus' name.

Father, let your favour make my work look good to the observers that will look at it, in Jesus' name.

Father, in your favour, let there be a positive turning in all my bad situations, in Jesus' name.

Father, let your favour turn my lack to abundance, in Jesus' name.

Father, let your favour purchase blessings that my righteousness can't purchase for me, in Jesus' name.

Father, let your favour grant me approval for every uncommon request I will make in any place, in Jesus' name.

Father, let your favour arrest for my sake all those handling my requests in all places, in Jesus' name.

Father, let your favour grant favourable, irreversible approval to all my applications, in Jesus' name.

Father, your favour will make me become accepted and celebrated wherever I operate, in Jesus' name.

Father, in your favour, blindfold all the faultfinders concerning my requests, in Jesus' name.

Father, let your favour be placed on every request I make in any place, a mark of divine approval, in Jesus' name.

Father, let your favour open my eyes to every supply that heaven will send me, in Jesus' name.

Father, I decree that in your favour, I shall only break through and not break down, in Jesus' name.

Father, let your favour strengthen me to claim each of the blessings you had allocated to me, in Jesus' name.

Father, in your favour, let there be safe delivery to me of all my allocated blessings, in Jesus' name.

Father, I decree that your favour will not let any of my miracles be given to another person, in Jesus' name.

Father, let your favour draw to serve me competent people who have the skills I don't have, in Jesus' name.

Father, because your favour is upon me, let every tree of non-achievement be rooted out of my life today, in Jesus' name.

Father, let your favour connect me to destiny connectors, in Jesus' name.

Father, I prophesy that the fragrance of your favour will draw people who will push me forward and serve me in pursuance of my dreams and visions, in Jesus' name.

Father, let your favour take me out of any meaningless relationship and bring me into a meaningful relationship, in Jesus' name.

Father, in your favour, let all those contaminating your anointing on my life be removed from me today, in Jesus' name.

Father, I prophesy that the fragrance of your favour will draw men of war to serve me and help me win all my battles, in Jesus' name.

Father, I prophesy that the fragrance of your favour will draw people that will serve me, add value to my life, and enrich it, in Jesus' name.

Father, I prophesy that the fragrance of your favour shall draw people who will serve me and fill every emptiness in my life with treasures, in Jesus' name.

Father, I prophesy that in any area of life where I had lost ground, your favour shall make me gain more ground than I had lost, in Jesus' name.

Father, I prophesy that the fragrance of your favour shall draw people who will serve me and have a genuine interest in my success, in Jesus' name.

Father, I declare that your favour shall never make me know disappointment anymore, in all my days, in Jesus' name.

Father, I prophesy that the fragrance of your favour shall draw to serve me people that will not rest until I win all my battles, in Jesus' name.

Father, in your favour, let every tormentor of my soul be permanently put in prison for my sake, in Jesus' name.

Father, I decree that in all my days, your favour shall make me never walk in perverted destiny any longer, in Jesus' name.

Father, I prophesy that the fragrance of your favour shall draw people that will serve me and cause heaven to open over my life permanently, in Jesus' name.

Father, I declare that your favour shall expose and defeat every hidden plan of the enemy concerning me, in Jesus' name.

Father, I prophesy that the fragrance of your favour shall draw to serve me people that will turn me into an achiever, in Jesus' name.

Father, in your favour, I decree a favourable transformation in every area of my life, in Jesus' name.

Father, I prophesy that in your favour towards me, every liar the devil has brought into my life shall be exposed and separated from me, in Jesus' name.

Father, I prophesy that your favour upon my life shall remove every threatening situation of my life far away from me, and I shall see them no more, in Jesus' name.

Father, in your favour towards me, I prophesy that whether the enemy likes it or not, I shall not live a wasted life, in Jesus' name.

Father, I prophesy into my life that this day, your favour shall grant me joy without limit over all that concerns me, in Jesus' name.

Father, I prophesy into my life this day that your favour shall grant me strength without limit, and I will never run out of strength, in Jesus' name.

Father, I prophesy into my life that this day, your favour shall grant me peace without limit and that my peace will always flow like a river, in Jesus' name.

Father, I prophesy into my life that this day, your favour shall grant me victory without limit and that I will never be defeated in all my days, in Jesus' name.

Father, I prophesy into my life that this day, your favour shall bring me good news without limit, and I will always have good news in all that concerns me, in Jesus' name.

Father, I prophesy into my life this day that your favour shall grant me enlargement without limit, and I will permanently enlarge in all areas of life, in Jesus' name.

Father, I prophesy into my life that this day, your favour shall grant me acceptance without limit and that wherever I go, I shall always experience acceptance, in Jesus' name.

Father, I prophesy into my life that this day, your favour shall grant me wisdom without limit and that I will always have the solution to every problem in my life, in Jesus' name.

Father, I prophesy into my life that this day, your favour shall grant me gains without limit and that I will always make profits in all my labour, in Jesus' name.

Father, I prophesy into my life that this day, your favour shall grant me support without limit, such that wherever I go, helpers will always be available to assist me, in Jesus' name.

Father, I prophesy that your favour will bring me to the right place at the right time for my miracles, in Jesus' name.

Father, I prophesy that your favour shall give me the right attitude on the day of my miracles, in Jesus' name.

Father, I prophesy that your favour shall quicken me on the day of my miracle, in Jesus' name.

Father, I prophesy that your favour shall disconnect me from everything in my past that wants to hinder my miracles, in Jesus' name.

Father, I prophesy that your favour shall close every distance and gap between me and my helpers of destiny, in Jesus' name.

Father, I declare prophetically that by your favour, I shall find every support I need from you to succeed in all I do, in Jesus' name.

Father, I declare prophetically that by your favour, I shall perform excellently in all my deeds, in Jesus' name.

Father, I declare prophetically that by your favour, I and all that is mine will enjoy your preservation, in Jesus' name.

Father, I declare prophetically that by your favour, every injustice I have suffered, you shall overturn, in Jesus' name.

Father, I prophesy that every evil word spoken to do me harm, your favour shall turn it around to do me good, in Jesus' name.

Father, I prophesy that every hidden treasure darkness has kept away from me, and your favour shall make it visible for me, in Jesus' name.

Father, I prophesy that your favour will turn my sickness to health, in Jesus' name.

Father, I prophesy that your favour will take me to the front, in every area of life, where I am behind, in Jesus' name.

Father, I prophesy that your favour will turn all my losses into gains for me, in Jesus' name.

Father, I prophesy that your favour will turn me into a prosperous man who always succeeds in all he does, in Jesus' name.

Father, I prophesy that your favour will make me skilful in success-making, in Jesus' name.

Father, I prophesy that your favour will multiply good things in my hands, in Jesus' name.

Father, I prophesy that your favour will make me noticeable to those who will appreciate and reward my potential, in Jesus' name.

Father, I prophesy that your favour will make me noticeable to those who will advertise my gifting to the world, in Jesus' name.

Father, I prophesy that for my sake, your favour will cancel every ungodly delay working against me in all places, in Jesus' name.

Father, I prophesy that your mercy will bring me unusual favour from desert places, in Jesus' name.

Father, I prophesy that your favour will close every door of oppression in my life, in Jesus' name.

Father, I prophesy that your favour will close every door, exposing me to the attack of spiritual robbers, in Jesus' name.

Father, I prophesy that your favour will close every door of frustration in my life, in Jesus's name.

Father, I prophesy that your favour will close every door of wasted efforts in my life, in Jesus' name.

Father, I prophesy that your favour will disappoint all those waiting for me to suffer for my error, in Jesus' name.

Father, I prophesy that your favour will put to shame all those who want to take advantage of my mistake to cheat me, in Jesus' name.

Father, I prophesy that your favour will reverse every irreversible mistake I have made, in Jesus' name.

Father, I prophesy that your favour will blindfold the world to all my errors, in Jesus' name.

Father, I prophesy that your favour will soften people's hearts towards me wherever I go, in Jesus' name.

Father, I prophesy that your favour will make people gentle towards me wherever I go, in Jesus' name.

Father, I prophesy that your favour will make me find kindness with people, in Jesus' name.

Father, I prophesy that your favour will make me find safety in the hands of people wherever I go, in Jesus' name.

Father, I prophesy that your favour will revoke every legal ground I had permitted the enemy to have against me, in Jesus' name.

Father, I prophesy that your favour will unseat for me every stranger I had permitted to sit on my seat of honour, in Jesus' name.

Father, I prophesy that your favour will claim for me every birthright I had given to the enemy, in Jesus' name.

Father, I prophesy that your favour will grant me success far greater than my effort, in Jesus' name.

Father, I prophesy that your favour will grant me possessions greater than my resources, in Jesus' name.

Father, I prophesy that your favour will grant me an appointment greater than my qualifications, in Jesus' name.

Father, I prophesy that your favour shall grant me a promotion greater than my performance, in Jesus' name.

Father, I prophesy that your favour will grant me a harvest greater than my sowing, in Jesus's name.

Father, I prophesy that your favour will grant me a reward greater than my labour, in Jesus' name.

Father, I prophesy that your favour will grant me direction greater than my wisdom, in Jesus' name.

Father, I prophesy that your favour will grant me fulfilment greater than my dream and vision, in Jesus' name.

Father, I prophesy that your favour will make me come out of all my troubles with a new song, in Jesus' name.

Father, I prophesy that your favour will grant me victory where I'm supposed to suffer defeat, in Jesus' name.

Father, I prophesy that your favour will grant me justification where I am supposed to suffer condemnation, in Jesus' name.

Father, I prophesy that your favour will grant me lifting where I'm supposed to be brought down, in Jesus' name.

Father, I prophesy that your favour will grant me courage where I am supposed to be under fear, in Jesus' name.

Father, I prophesy that your favour will grant me dominance where I should be, in Jesus' name.

Father, I prophesy that your favour will grant me an increase where I am supposed to suffer a decrease, in Jesus' name.

Father, I prophesy that your favour will grant me achievements that will enforce acceptance, in Jesus' name.

Father, I prophesy that your favour will cancel every judgment written against me in any place, in Jesus' name.

Father, I prophesy that your favour will cancel every demonic claim over my life, in Jesus' name.

Father, I prophesy that your favour will make possible for me what my mistake has made impossible for me, in Jesus' name.

Father, I prophesy that your favour will frustrate every target of the enemy in my life, in Jesus' name.

Father, I prophesy that in your favour, you will unfold my set time for favour today, in Jesus' name.

Father, I prophesy that in your favour, you will help me to create a space for me at the top, in Jesus' name.

Father, I prophesy that you will change my level in Jesus' name in your favour.

Father, I prophesy that in your favour, you will give me my own territory—my own space, in Jesus' name.

Father, I prophesy that in your favour, you will put me in command of all situations of my life, in Jesus' name.

Father, I prophesy that in your favour, you will make my word a law that can't be disobeyed, in Jesus' name.

Father, I prophesy that in your favour, you will make me the head, not the tail, in Jesus' name.

Father, I prophesy that in your favour, you will make me a person of importance wherever I go, in Jesus' name.

Father, I prophesy that your favour will bring me to the place of many possibilities, in Jesus' name.

Father, I prophesy that in your favour, you will deliver me from every temptation, in Jesus' name.

Father, I prophesy that in your favour, you will make your ways known to me, in Jesus' name.

Father, I prophesy that in your favour, you will connect me to champions to make me a champion, in Jesus' name.

Father, I prophesy that in your favour, you will give me a heart that receives divine illumination in every decision I make, in Jesus' name.

Father, I prophesy that in your favour, you will help me reach my goals in all I do, in Jesus' name.

Father, I prophesy that in your favour, you will create around me conducive conditions that will make me succeed in all my plans, in Jesus' name.

Father, I prophesy that in your favour, you will supply every resource I need for my plan to succeed, in Jesus' name.

Father, I prophesy that in your favour, you will supervise every situation concerning my plans to make it succeed, in Jesus' name.

Father, I prophesy that your favour will make me conquer all my struggles, in Jesus' name.

Father, I prophesy that your favour will make me press on against all odds, in Jesus' name.

Father, I prophesy that your favour will make me unstoppable to every resistance, in Jesus' name.

Books From the Same Author

Journey to the Next Level

The New Creature

Building a Glorious Home:
A Pathway to a Successful Marriage

Enemy of Marriage

Words That Heal

The Winning Formula

Faith that Always wins

Common Mistakes Parents make about their Children

Recovery is Possible
When you are desperate for a miracle

Decision
Path way to a wise decision making

Stop your fear before it stops you

The Visionary

30 Covenant Right Prayers of Declaration That Can Change Your Life

A-Z Practices That Can Preserve Your Marriage

This book, and all these other books from the same author, are available at Christian bookstores and distributors worldwide.

They can also be obtained through online retail partners such as Amazon or by contacting the author at the address below:

Address: 21-23 Stokes Croft, Bristol BS1 3PY United Kingdom

Email: kkasali@yahoo.com

Telephone: +44 (0) 7727 159 581

www.ingramcontent.com/pod-product-compliance
Lightning Source LLC
Chambersburg PA
CBHW061738070526
44585CB00024B/2728